THE KIDS' BOOK OF
FISHING

Written and Illustrated
by Michael J. Rosen

WORKMAN PUBLISHING • NEW YORK

Acknowledgments

Although there are many books and agencies that helped to form this book, most valuable in its writing have been the hours spent in the company of two families: childhood summers with my own family and more recent summers with the Gaspers. And since so much of the joy in fishing comes from generations of such sharing, this book is dedicated to that next generation of anglers: my nephew Benjamin Rosen and Alexander and Zachary Gasper.

Special thanks, too, to Michael Pirtle who first cast the idea for such a book, to Sallie Gouverneur who took the bait, and to Anne Kostick who ran with it.

Rosen, Michael J., 1954–
  The kids' book of fishing by Michael J. Rosen.
    p. cm.
  Summary: A beginner's guide to fishing that discusses fish varieties, basic techniques, and equipment, with an emphasis on freshwater catch-and-release fishing. Packaged with each book are thirty feet of line, hooks, sinkers, and related equipment.
  ISBN 0-89480-866-4
  1. Fishing—Juvenile literature.
[1. Fishing.] I. Title.
SH445.R67 1991
799.1—dc20   91-7517
                                        CIP
                                         AC

Front cover illustrations by Jenny Campbell and David Biedrzycki Book and back cover illustrations by Michael J. Rosen

Workman Publishing Company, Inc.
708 Broadway
New York, NY 10003

Manufactured in the United States of America
10 9 8 7 6 5 4

CONTENTS

THE NEVER-ENDING STORY OF FISHING

Everywhere on Earth, wherever there is water, people are fishing. And people have been fishing those waters since the beginning of human time. Except for a few changes from the handmade to the store-bought, fishing is pretty much the same as it was for the first people who threaded an angleworm on a hook and gave us the word "angler."

Fish haven't changed much. The fish you might find in nearby waters are like the fish that might be found thousands of miles away, or many years ago.

Bait hasn't changed much, either. We modern anglers have fancier lures, plastic worms, and other newfangled tricks, but even the earliest anglers had their own fishing tricks—hand-carved lures, and lines weighted with rocks or small bags of sand.

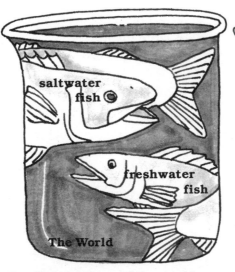

In all the waters of the world, there are 32,000 kinds of fish. Two-thirds of them live in salt water, and one-third live in fresh water.

Have the places where anglers go fishing changed? Sadly, there is less and less clean, clear water for fish or for fishing. And many species have experienced stunted growth or

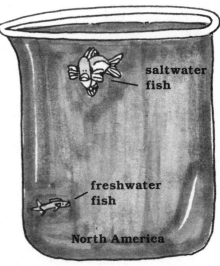

Of all these fish, only 3,200 kinds live in North America, and only 712 of them live in fresh water.

extinction. Still, the complicated liquid where fish live is nearly the same.

What an angler knows about the water hasn't changed very much. You are still fishing in

THE FISH YOU'RE FISHING FOR

Fish have swum the oceans for 400 million years. The very first fish were heavily armored, jawless (they sucked in food), and spent all their time on the bottom of the ocean. Once fish developed jaws, they could seek out tougher, larger food and begin to swim freely through the water searching for prey.

the dark (water), and still tangling with an invisible, different intelligence beneath the surface. Every angler must learn to "read" the water in order to find, attract, and outthink this cagey challenger.

For all our computerized depth finders, high-powered motorboats, and automatic reels, people are still tossing some kind of food into the water and hoping the fish will bite. And hoping hasn't changed at all.

The one real advantage you have over earlier anglers is that you can learn and use everything they worked so hard to find out. And all you observe and experience every time you fish will add to your knowledge.

When you take your hand-line or your fishing pole or your spinning rod down to the water, you join the anglers in the next lake and the next state, the anglers of the last century, and probably the anglers in the next one. Fishing is like one story told all over the world—and when you add your fishing line, it becomes a new line in that story, connecting with all the lines that have already been cast.

Fishing is a sport in which you compete with yourself. Winning in the sport of fishing is a matter of enjoyment. Enjoying the day, the weather, the scenery, the company, and of course, the challenge. Did you cast your bait in the right spot, attract the fish with your lure, release the fish unharmed? That's how you win on a day of fishing.

So welcome to the oldest unofficial club on Earth. All that's needed to be a member is a promise to follow all regulations, respect for other anglers and for your environment, and a commitment to being safe and careful in every way.

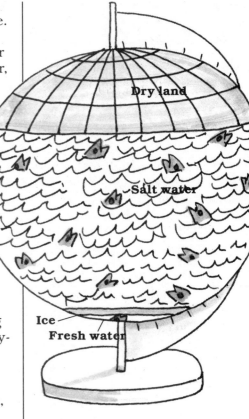

Three-fourths of our planet is under water; only one-fourth is dry land. But saltwater oceans make up 97 percent of Earth's water. Another 2 percent of the water is frozen in the polar ice caps. It is only the remaining 1 percent that is fresh water— all the lakes and rivers and ponds and streams. And that 1 percent provides a home for all freshwater creatures.

YOU AND THE FISH
PART ONE

Every time you fish, you have a chance to enjoy, observe, and even change a watery, mysterious world. The more you learn about fish and their environment, the better angler you can be. You'll find the best ways of catching fish, and the best ways of assuring that fish will always be swimming in our waters.

Make a simple hand-line with the contents of THE KIDS' TACKLE BOX. Discover the perfect fishing hole, bait up, and cast: What happens next is between you and the fish!

YOUR PART IN THE BIG PICTURE

One out of every four people in America claims to be a part-time angler. That's 60 million people. Just as fast as our human population grows (which means more and more anglers), our natural resources shrink (which means less shoreline, fewer lakes and streams, less fields and forests). Much of the remaining water that hasn't been bulldozed, drained, or rerouted has become polluted from agricultural run-off, industrial wastes, and chemical spillage.

Fish are very vulnerable. Changes in their environment can seriously affect them. Is there water deep enough to keep the fish cool in summer? Are there enough places to hide and to lay eggs? Is there enough oxygen to breathe and food to eat? Are there too many of one kind of fish or too few of another to have a natural balance?

As a new angler, you play a

key part in preserving the resources—fish and all other wildlife—of our threatened planet. Anglers everywhere have begun to realize the increasing need for regulations that protect fish and their environments. As a careful angler you should:

◀ know the legal number of fish you are permitted to catch in a given season and on a given day. This ensures there will be enough of that

fish for successful breeding and for anglers to catch in the future.

◀ know which kinds and which sizes of fish are legal to catch. State laws protect species that are suffering from poor breeding conditions, overfishing, or disease.

◀ follow your state's fishing laws, unless you are fishing on private property. Any tackle shop, license bureau, or county extension office will have lists of seasonal limits. Since it is hard to enforce fishing laws, every angler makes a private pledge to abide by state laws and to respect the land and water where he or she fishes.

Catch-and-Release Fishing

Many states have a rule that, at certain fishing spots, all fish must be immediately released after landing. This is called catch-and-release fishing. Anglers use the smallest hooks that will do the job, and they remove the hook's barb to protect the fish.

Many anglers have decided that catch-and-release is the only kind of fishing for them. In their minds, this is a more honest and fair sport. It's more exciting. It's more respectful of the fish and the ecosystem—which is the total environment of animals, plants, minerals, and climate that make up one particular place. For vegetarians who do not eat meat of any

kind, releasing fish is the only right and ethical thing to do. And for anglers who plan a great day of adventure but who don't want to transport, clean, and cook a fish, catch-and-release is the responsible way to fish.

Everyone must practice some catch-and-release fishing. When an undersized, endangered, or out-of-season fish is hooked, it must be safely released. So prepare for catch-and-release

fishing. Learn how to properly release a fish (page 28 tells you how to do this), and how to remove the barb from your hook (page 34 shows how to make a barbless hook). A barbless hook is less likely to harm a fish when it is being hooked or un-hooked. It's an extra challenge; some anglers admit they lose a few more fish that squirm free of a barbless hook. But developing real skill is part of the fun of fishing.

Learn the safe way to catch and release a fish.

THINK LIKE A FISH

The smarter you are about fish, the smarter you'll be about fishing. Since you can't exactly outswim the fish, you'll need to outwit, out-guess, and outsmart them. Here are a few basic facts about fish: how they move; how they perceive the watery world around them; what they eat.

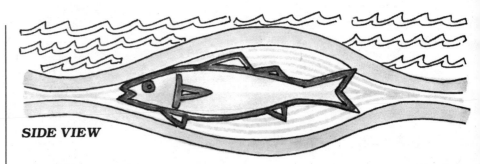

SIDE VIEW

The basic fish shape slices through water; it doesn't shove against water. Unlike a human body, a fish's body is one sleek shape; head, body and tail aren't as clearly separated.

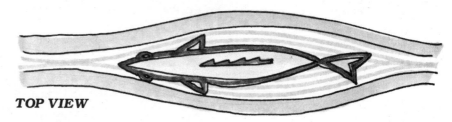

TOP VIEW

Fishy Moves: How a Fish Gets Around

All fish live underwater. Their bodies are built for swimming. To do this, a fish's body is streamlined, shaped to slide swiftly through water without pushing against it. Streamlining makes fish pointed rather than blunt, long rather than tall, and narrow rather than wide.

EIGHT FINS AND A FLOAT
The tail of the fish is the **caudal fin**. This is the fish's propeller and it provides the power. Waving back and forth, the tail paddles water side to side, sending the fish forward.

To go backward, a fish uses its paired fins: the **pectoral fins**, which are the fish's arms, and the **pelvic** or **ventral fins**, which are the fish's legs.

Working together, these paired fins will also move the fish forward, up, or down. They can also hold the fish in the same spot by treading water, and stop the fish by fanning open away from the body.

A fish has unpaired fins, too. The **dorsal fin** is the large, stiff, spiny fin running down the fish's back; some fish have more than one. The dorsal fin keeps the fish from tipping over

FISH ANATOMY

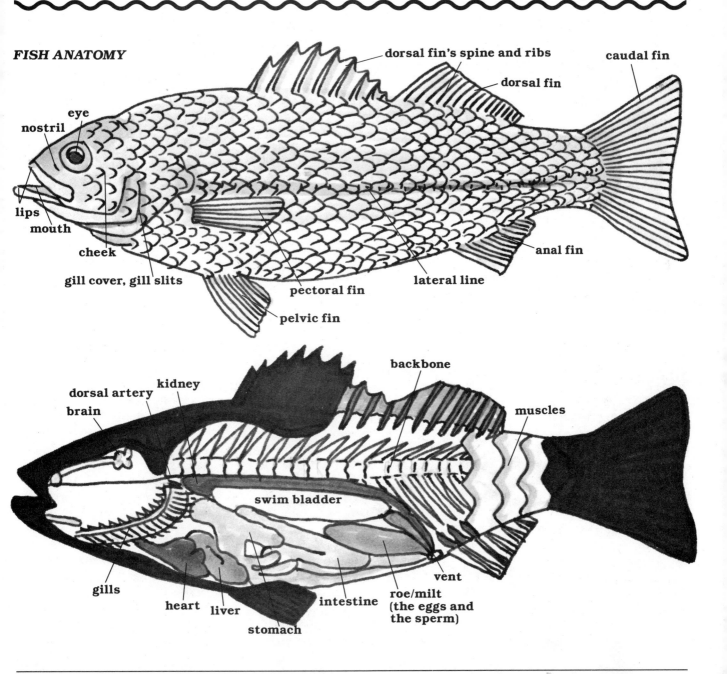

Think of a fish as two rowboats linked up with one motorboat: two oars toward the front, two oars toward the rear, and one propeller in the back.

or turning upside down. It is not as bendable as the paired fins.

Under the fish's belly, toward its tail, is the **anal fin**. Some fish, like salmon and trout, have an **adipose fin**, located on the back between the dorsal fin and the tail. These fins help with braking and balancing.

A fish also uses its **swim bladder** to rise and to sink. A fish forces air into this organ and, like an air bubble, it floats the fish upward. When the fish forces air out of the swim bladder, the bubble shrinks and the fish sinks downward.

Breathing Underwater

A fish breathes by taking oxygen from water just as all land dwellers breathe by taking oxygen from air. Since both air and water contain many things besides oxygen, it's the job of the gills and lungs to extract only the oxygen.

A stream of water is sucked in through the fish's mouth and forced out again through its gill slits. A fish's "lungs" or gills, are located beneath the gill cover, a flap of protective skin. The gills themselves are red from the many blood vessels that lie just under the surface. As water passes over the feathery projections of the gills, the tiny blood vessels extract the oxygen.

FISH NEVER STOP GROWING

Birds and mammals stop growing when they reach their full

A FISH CAN DROWN IN AIR OR WATER

When you bring a fish out of water, it begins to drown just as you would drown if you tried to inhale water. Water in your lungs is deadly; air in a fish's gills is just as deadly.

But a fish can also drown in water. If there are no streams or springs, no rain or melting snow to replenish the water, a lake or river's oxygen can be used up. If there are no winds or waves to whip air into the water, if pollutants create surface scum, or if a heavy cover of water lilies seals off the surface, the water will stagnate and become lifeless.

adult size. Fish continue to grow longer and wider and heavier their whole life. As a rule of thumb, the older the fish, the bigger the fish.

Let's say you found two fish from different lakes, but of the same age and the same species—for instance, a pair of three-year-old largemouth bass. The one from the larger lake would likely be larger than the one from the smaller lake. The bigger the body of water, the bigger the fish can grow, since there's likely to be more food available in the larger body of water for the fish to eat.

Fish Chow: What Do Fish Eat?

Young fish eat plankton, the tiniest plant and animal life. As a fish grows, it eats larger and larger foods. Some fish eat only plants; some eat smaller fish; some eat crabs, snails, or squids; and some eat frogs and salamanders, or even mammals such as mice or baby seals.

Some fish, like wrass, bass, and perch, have teeth in their throat to help chew their food. Some fish, like pike and blue-fish, have real—and sharp!—teeth along their jaws.

A fish's teeth are not meant for chewing. They are built to seize and hold food. Their throats do the chewing and their stomachs do the digesting.

Finding Food: A Fish's Six Senses

A fish searches for food with all its senses—five that humans also possess, and one extraordinary one. If you can understand what a fish senses, then you're better equipped to outsmart it.

A FISH-EYE VIEW

A fish can see several feet in water, especially in clear water. And it can see into the air above the water. If a fish sees an angler on the bank or leaning over the water, it will often make a mad dash to hide. Anglers fishing in streams always walk upstream, against the current, so they can sneak up on the fish, which are facing upstream. Fish that live in deeper, darker water have a reflective surface at the rear of their eyeballs to help them see. This brightens the little sunlight that does reach that depth.

Catfish often live in water so muddy that their eyes barely

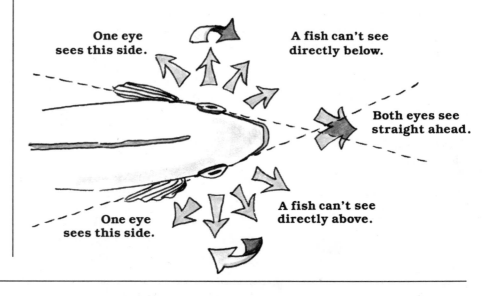

One eye sees this side.

A fish can't see directly below.

Both eyes see straight ahead.

One eye sees this side.

A fish can't see directly above.

Instead of swimming upright, it begins to swim sideways. Over a period of weeks, the eye continues moving and the fish continues leaning until the flounder has both eyes on its top side. When you hook a flounder, you can feel its odd sideways weight as you reel it in.

When the young flounder is about an inch long, its bottom eye begins to move around to the top side! And the fish starts leaning, then tipping over.

see. Like a sightless person who taps a cane when walking, a catfish uses long "whiskers," called barbels, around its mouth to "see." As the fish combs the murky bottom, the barbels feel out—and actually taste—hidden bits of food.

A flounder is born with one eye on each side of its head, like most fish. But because an adult flounder lives on the ocean floor, changing colors to match the bottom, both of its eyes face up.

A fish's eyes have no eyelids. They are always open. Even when a fish sleeps—and not many fish sleep—its eyes are wide open.

AN UNDERWATER NOSE
A fish does have a nose but it doesn't breathe through it. A fish's two nostrils, located on its snout, are nearly invisible and are used only for smelling.

A fish's sense of smell isn't nearly as strong as a dog's, but it does help locate food. In fact, some anglers use special scents to attract fish. Bait stores stock many bottled scents that are supposed to make your lures more delicious-smelling to fish.

WHAT A FISH HEARS
Fish can hear, but you'll never locate an outer ear. Sound travels very quickly through water and for very long distances. Sound waves strike a fish's

skull and these vibrations travel directly to the inner ear. Fish are certainly able to pick out the sound from the air, too.

A FISH'S SIXTH SENSE: THE LATERAL LINE
Fish have one more sense on their side. Through it, they can half-feel and half-hear vibrations, locate food or predators, orient themselves in currents, and detect changes in water temperature and pressure. This sense is contained within the **lateral line**, a slightly darker stripe that runs down each side. (You can see these stripes on some fish.)

The lateral line is especially sensitive to nearby, low-frequency vibrations, such as footsteps on the riverbank or something dropped on the water's surface. You can talk, sing, or play a radio very softly and not startle most fish. But if you move something that connects with the water—bounce on the dock, tumble rocks down the bank, or lift your minnow bucket from the water—you'll be announcing to all nearby fish: "Attention, everyone. Clumsy angler about to cast. Clear the area."

Fish-to-Fish Communication

Some fish make sounds. Anglers often hear spots grunt and croakers croak. Other fish seem to toot, whistle, burp, or squeak. Most of these sounds are produced by muscles surrounding their swim bladders.

But this isn't really speaking. The language of fish is instinct —built-in actions and reactions. Fish communication is what one fish understands about another fish's movements and colors.

Some fish swim in "schools," keeping the same distance apart, turning precisely at the same time. How the group coordinates these movements is mysterious and strange, but each fish's lateral lines play a part.

Other fish don't synchronize movements, but they do combine efforts when hunting or feeding. This friendlier club is called a "shoal" of fish. It, too, requires some kind of communication among members.

What Can a Fish Feel?

With a few exceptions—the catfish family, for instance—a fish's body is covered with scales. Whatever scales cover the fish at birth remain throughout its life, though lost scales are replaced. These permanent scales provide some protection for a fish, but it is a flimsy armor.

A PAINFUL SUBJECT?

Since fish do not have pain receptors in their scales, they don't have a sense of touch the way you and I think of it. The fish's brain doesn't interpret pain.

A fish's lips don't have these pain detectors, either. When your hook pierces its lip, the fish's brain doesn't feel this as agony or hurt. The fish isn't suffering. It simply knows that something is pulling it, keeping it from swimming free. A roughly torn lip might keep the fish from eating, and a deeply swallowed hook might permanently harm the fish, but an angler works to avoid that.

Anglers don't feel that fishing is a cruel sport. They understand that fish are not sensitive creatures capable of real suffering.

THE SCALES OF A FISH

Like a clam's shell or a tree trunk's rings, a fish's scales grow in rings that will reveal its age. Narrow rings indicate winters, a time of slow growth. Wider rings indicate summers, a time of warmer water, more food, and faster growth.

A fish's scale is also like a fingerprint: Each kind of fish has a unique scale. People who study fish can identify a fish from just one of its scales.

WHERE TO FISH

There are fish to be found under the frozen waters of the North and South poles, in the steamy swamps of the tropics, in high mountain currents that rush past fish at amazing speeds, and in the deepest trenches of the ocean where the pressure is 1,000 times greater than at the surface. And some anglers might be interested in trying to catch some of those fish.

But one kind of fish or another is likely to be living a short walk or drive from where *you* live.

Fishing Holes and Even Larger Bodies of Water

If you've visited a nearby lake, bay, creek, stream, reservoir, or river, you've probably already found at least one good place to try your luck fishing. A map of your immediate area is likely to show several other good spots. Most state parks have fishing and boating areas. It's also a good idea to check:

Other anglers and tackle shops for their favorite spots.

Fishing magazines and newspapers. Find them at

your library or bookstore. A few are sure to be geared to your region and will list nearby places and local strategies.

Your state's department of wildlife and fisheries, or a county extension service. There might be a local chapter of the Isaak Walton League or other fishing organizations. Summer camps, scouting clubs, and recreation centers often have outings and programs for local anglers.

Bodies of water located on private property—the grounds of a local corporation, housing complex, office park, or golf course, for example—are often available to anglers. You simply

need permission. Usually, a phone call or a letter will get you the go-ahead.

Country homes and farms often have a stream or pond on their property. Some people even stock their ponds with fish—partly to limit plant and algae growth, but also so the family anglers might have something good to catch. Present yourself to the property owners ahead of time and ask permission. Assure them that you will respect their property and observe whatever limits they would like to impose. You might even offer to share the day's catch.

If there are houses built along a lake or ocean, ask permission from the owners before fishing from their shore. They don't own the water or the fish, but they might own the land and you don't want to trespass.

There might even be pay-ponds in your area. These ponds are heavily stocked with certain fish. You pay an admission fee for a one-day fishing pass. Pay-ponds might be good for practice, and a sure bet for dinner fish, but it's a little like fishing in an overstocked aquarium. You lose a bit of the adventure of finding and outwitting the fish, and you lose some-

thing of the peace and quiet and mystery of nature.

Beware of Fishing in Polluted Waters

Many streams and creeks and ponds and lakes of America are in danger because of litter and dumping, so the places you might choose to fish could be polluted. It might even be unsafe to eat the fish swimming there—that is, if fish have even survived. Learn to recognize signs of polluted water. Don't fish where the water is:

Very green. When algae are too abundant, the water's oxygen content is very low. Algae will thicken and cloud the water, making it hard for much else to live there.

Cloudy and muddy. Fish can't breathe if too much dirt is

Wherever you decide to fish, wear a lightweight life jacket. State laws will insist on life jackets in any boat if you are under a certain age (usually sixteen). But it's a good idea to wear a life jacket any place you fish if:

⊱ you are not a strong, accomplished swimmer;

⊱ you are fishing near or in a stream with a fast-moving current;

⊱ you are fishing from a steep bank or a slippery slope where it would be easy to lose your footing;

⊱ you are casting into deep water from a dock or a bridge.

Another important safety measure is a fishing buddy. It is always best to be with someone else when you are fishing, in case of emergency.

churned up in the water. In healthy water, plant life keeps the dirt settled. Don't choose a spot with muddy water and few plants around its banks.

Shiny with scum or a film of color on the surface. A colorful film on a pond could mean leaking sewage or oil. (Motorboats often leak gasoline; this contributes to pollution, but won't cause a major surface film.) Sometimes a water's surface becomes so spread with oily pollutants that the oil will coat a fish's gills and prevent it from breathing.

Orange or red. A surface coating of these colors signals real pollution: a factory dumping chemicals, run-off from a landfill, or industrial spillage.

Foamy, sudsy, or frothy. Soapy bubbles may be produced from detergents, rinses, and chemicals, not one of which belongs in a living ecosystem. (Waterfalls and rushing water will produce a foamy water full of oxygen. That's not a pollutant; it's a prime place for fish!)

Awful smelling, especially if the smell resembles rotten eggs. Aside from being an unpleasant place to fish, that smell could signal leaking sewage. Germs from sewers can kill wildlife, and even the animals that survive such poisons can become poisonous for other creatures—like us—to eat.

Many other kinds of pollutants are not so easily spotted. Some power plants dump heated water into lakes, making the natural water too hot for the creatures that live there. The run-off from lawn fertilizers and manure from cattle and other livestock are also toxic to fish. Chemicals dissolved in water can directly harm a fish (by poisoning), kill its food (causing starvation), or keep it from laying eggs that will hatch.

Fish in water that sparkles with life! Look for a surface full of bugs, plants, and jumping fish. Look for shallow water where you can see minnows, frogs, and plants. And look for a place where people are already fishing. That's a sure sign of healthy, unpolluted water.

GETTING STARTED

Now that you know something about fish, you're almost ready to try your luck at catching one. There are many ways to catch fish, and lots of fish-catching equipment, but a basic "rig" is not very complicated. You need something to attract a fish (bait or lures), something to catch hold of a fish (a hook), something light and flexible that will dangle the bait and hook where the fish will see it (a line), and something that helps you hold on to the line (a pole or stick).

The *Kids' Tackle Box* that comes with THE KIDS' BOOK OF FISHING contains basic fishing tackle, as well as a few other items to get you started.

Line: 30 feet of 6-pound test monofilament line, which means you can catch up to a 6-pound fish on this line without breaking it. The line is colored yellow to make it more visible while you're fishing.

Hooks: Two #6 hooks (the small ones), for most small and small-mouthed fish. One #1/0 hook for bigger fish.

Bobber: This red-and-white plastic ball hooks on to your line and will signal you when a fish is nibbling or biting your bait.

Weights: Three BB-size, split-shot lead sinkers, which clamp on the line to keep the bait hanging down below the surface in a pond.

One "plummet" weight, which can help you find the correct depth for your bait, and can keep your bait below the surface in a moving stream.

Swivel: The swivel lets your lure spin around without twisting the line. The loop end attaches to the line, and the snap end holds the lure.

With these items, a stick, and bait, you'll be ready to fish. The sections that follow will show you how to combine this tackle into a hand-line, or on a rig for pole fishing (see page 26), jigging (see page 27), or rod-and-reel fishing (see page 58).

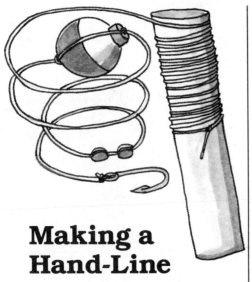

Making a Hand-Line

A hand-line is the most basic fishing gear. It's a hook, line, sinker, and (sometimes) bobber. It's a fishing pole without the pole. A hand-line is easiest to use if attached to a strong, smooth, short stick (about 6 inches long), such as a thick dowel, or part of an old broom handle or fallen tree branch (peel off the bark to make a smooth surface).

ASSEMBLING YOUR HAND-LINE

1. Cut about 20 feet of line.

2. Attach one end of the line to your smooth stick. Make a tight double-knot 2 inches from the end.

3. Attach a #6 hook to the other end of the line, using the clinch knot (see page 21).

4. Pinch on one or two split-shot sinkers. (Use two with the larger hook or if you are fishing in strong current. You want to keep the bait down.) To attach the split-shot sinker, use pliers. About 10 inches above the hook, slide the fishing line between the sinker's two halves. Then squeeze the two halves together with pliers.

5. Add your bobber, find your depth, bait your hook, and get ready to fish.

ATTACHING THE BOBBER

1. Push down the edge of the plug at the top, which will expose the top hook.

2. Slide your line beneath it,

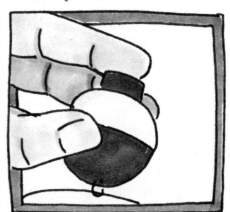

then release the plug to close the top hook in place.

3. Now slide your bobber where you want it to rest on your line.

4. To engage the bottom hook, put your finger over the top hook and plug and push in until the lower hook is opened. Slide your line under the lower hook, and release the plug. Now the bobber should be attached at two ends so it won't slide on your line.

Many bobbers have only one plug. A single hook holds the line in place.

The Plummet: Depth Finder

You're on the bank, you're ready to cast, but first you need

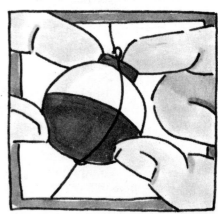

TIE THE CLINCH KNOT

1. Slide 2 inches of line through the hook's eye. Twist the end of the line five or six times around itself.

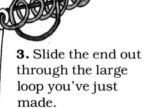

2. Thread the end through the loop closest to the hook's eye.

3. Slide the end out through the large loop you've just made.

4. Now, an old angling secret: Take a little spit from your mouth and dab it on the loop. This helps to tighten the knot. Pull the end of the line to close the knot.

5. Clip any extra line with fingernail clippers.

to know how deep the water is where you're fishing. You could be fishing a spot that's far too shallow for the fish you're trying to catch. Or you might be trying to reach a bottom-dweller like a catfish but have your bobber set so that the bait hangs yards above the fish. To figure out where the bottom is, use your bobber and your plummet.

Tie the plummet to the end of your line using a surgeon's knot (see page 35). Now guess how deep the water will be where you want to land your cast—5 feet, 7 feet, 10 feet? Attach your bobber that many feet from the end of the plummet. Now cast your line to that spot and look carefully at your bobber (see illustration below).

Reel in, remove the plummet, tie on your hook or lure, and bait up. You should already have your sinker weights attached.

Is the bobber underwater? The water is deeper than you thought. Reset the bobber farther away from the plummet.

Is the bobber lying on its side? The water is shallower than you thought. Move the bobber closer to the plummet.

Is the bobber floating straight up and down in the water with its tip just poking above the surface? Then the plummet is resting right on the bottom. If you plan to bottom fish, you're all set. If you want the bait to float above the bottom, then slide the bobber closer to the plummet.

Bait your hook according to what's biting. Bass or catfish want a bigger mouthful. Using a larger (#1/0) hook, "gob" worms on the hook. Poke the point of the hook two or three times through two or three worms.

Bluegills, crappies, or sunfish need a smaller (#6) hook and a single worm threaded along the hook. Insert the hook's point into the worm and slide it inside the body of the worm until most of the hook's shank is covered.

If nibblers are stealing your worms but not taking your hook, use only a small piece of worm, cover the hook, and don't leave any worm to dangle free.

Hooked on Nightcrawlers

There are probably hundreds of useful baits in the world, but one thing all good bait must have in common is "fish appeal."

Nightcrawlers are the most popular bait in town. Though they are fairly inexpensive, there's no reason why you can't catch your own. Nightcrawlers are worms that like to go out for a little night air, especially after a heavy rain. You can create a heavy rain if the clouds haven't: Drench a corner of your lawn with the garden hose for a couple of nights in a row.

After dark, walk out to your "nightcrawler farm" and shine a flashlight on the ground. Nightcrawlers are sensitive to bright light, so use a rubber band to hold a piece of red or yellow tissue paper or cellophane over the light.

Usually, a nightcrawler keeps its tail in a burrow. When startled, the worm retreats—and fast!—into that hole. Snatch the worm before it can anchor itself in the burrow.

Using a little sawdust on your finger will make the nightcrawler less slippery. Keep

a little bag of sawdust in your pocket, and dip into it between worms. Then grab the nightcrawler as near to its hole as you can. Pull quickly, before the worm anchors itself. If the worm is already resisting, try this bird-tested trick: Tug steadily, then stop tugging (but don't let go), and then, once the worm relaxes, yank quickly.

Carry your worms in a paper carry-out food container, emptied cottage-cheese container, or other small compartment with a lid. Moss or dead leaves sprinkled with water make the best bedding for them, but use rainwater or lake water—tap water contains harmful chlorine.

If you need to store your

worms for a day or two, keep them in a refrigerator, in a cool basement, or in a cooler along with a zip-lock bag of ice.

You're likely to come across smaller worms, like leafworms and red worms, in your hunting. They make fine bait, especially for smaller fish. You can also find these worms under rocks, wet leaf piles, and felled logs—almost any place where the ground is covered and moisture can collect.

Casting Your Hand-Line

With a hand-line, you can cast very simply by just holding one end of the stick with one hand, and using the other hand to

toss the bait over the water. The best "pitch" is to hold the line right above your sinkers, and gently toss. Rather than underhand or overhand, use a sidehand toss: Send the line over the water with a gentle swing parallel to the ground.

If you are in a spot crowded with trees or other anglers, try this cast: Wind your fishing line neatly around one end of

your stick, starting at the knot and moving up toward the tip. Stop winding when you reach the weight or bobber. Hold the line in place with your thumb. Now swing the stick underhand, and release your thumb as soon as your hand begins pointing at the water. Continue your swing until your hand points straight out over the water. The line will unwrap and drop neatly into the water.

When you reel in a hand-line, hold the stick in both hands and turn it, rolling the line around the stick as you'd wind in a kite.

Every time you cast, you'll need to gauge the right force to use. Toss your line over the water too hard and you may watch the bait fly off ahead of the hook. Free lunch! Always use an even, deliberate swing. Skill, smoothness, and accuracy are more important than power.

How to Tell When You Have a Bite

Most often, you won't see the fish come up to your hook and inspect your bait. So how do you tell when you've got a bite? First and foremost, that is your bobber's job. Ordinarily, it just bobs gently on the surface. Current will jostle it, wind will

jiggle it, and you'll learn to distinguish those movements from the motions that signal a fish's presence. Some fish will nibble at the bait, or poke and prod it, before really taking the bait and running. The bobber will flutter or quiver and small ripples will spread in a circle

from the spot. The bobber might twitch, or tap the surface like a Morse code message. (It *is* a message, after all.) An experienced angler can read these signs.

When the fish takes the bait, or strikes, the bobber delivers a more urgent message. If you've kept your line taut, the first real tug on that line means business. Fish business! Depending upon the kind and size of the fish, the bobber might jerk, bounce, dart, jump, or sink. It might slide across the surface, dribble like a basketball, or zip underwater. Then it's time to stop watching the bobber and set the hook.

How to Set the Hook

If you feel the fish has taken your bait into its mouth, let the hook do its work. A quick, deliberate tug on the fishing line will bring the point of the hook through the fish's lip. That jerking motion must be strong enough to let the hook pierce, but not so hard as to tear the lip or yank the bait from its mouth. If your tug meets with another tug, you have secured the fish on your line. If the line continues to resist as you reel in, the fish is still there. You'll learn to feel the bite of each kind of fish: a trout's strike and run, a bass's sudden chomp, the fluttering of a nibbling carp, the light pull of a bluegill.

Landing a Fish

To keep your fish on the line, here are a couple of pointers:

Keep your line taut. If the line goes slack (looks loose and wobbly), the fish can often work the hook out by swimming in a different direction.

Let your line out a bit. If the fish runs with the bait (if it pulls hard away from you), you don't want your line to break. With your hand-line, loosen your grip on the stick and let the line feed out slowly.

Try to bring the fish toward shore as soon as it will let you. Pull it in at a medium speed by steadily turning the stick of your hand-line so that the fish comes closer and closer.

In very shallow water, you can beach the fish. Simply reel the fish closer to shore until you can reach into the water to grasp it. Then begin your quick release (see page 28).

HOW TO

MAKE A LANDING NET

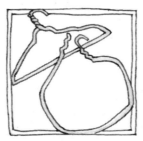 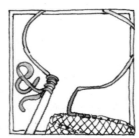 

You can make a net that will be strong enough for small- and medium-size fish. You'll need:

- 🐟 a strong wire hanger or other stiff wire

- 🐟 strong twine (5 feet)

- 🐟 a handle for the net (broom handle, tent pole, or dead tree limb that is thick, sturdy, and straight)

- 🐟 a mesh or string sack, preferably the large size used to hold onions or potatoes

1. Untwist and straighten the coat hanger or wire. You might need pliers or an adult's help to do this. Be careful of the wire's ends.

2. Reshape the wire into a hoop. Take the twine and bind one end of the wire to your handle. Wrap the twine many times around the wire and handle. Tie several double knots.

3. Thread the free end of the wire through the opening of the mesh sack. Weave it in and out so that it becomes the net's rim.

4. Now tie the free end of the wire to the handle. Again wind twine around the handle and wire, making a secure binding. Tie several double knots and cut off any extra twine.

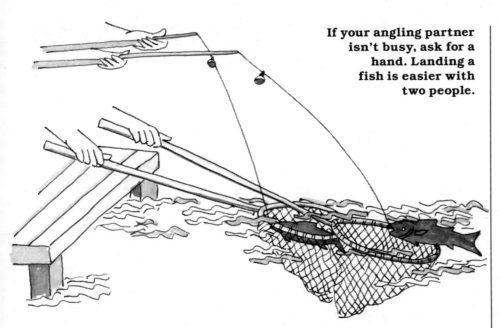

If your angling partner isn't busy, ask for a hand. Landing a fish is easier with two people.

The easiest way to land a fish is with a net (it's the only way if you are fishing from a boat, a dock, or a steep bank). You should not jerk the fish out of the water and leave it dangling in the air. This could break your line, lose the fish, or even injure someone—like yourself.

Hold your hand-line or rod with one hand, and grab the net with the other hand. Slide the landing net under the water in front of the fish, then slide it beneath the fish by pushing out the net and at the same time lifting up your line.

Once the fish is in the pocket of the net, bring the net toward you until it is within reach. Set down your line and use your free hand to remove the hook. Use the mesh of the net to help grip the fish.

Attaching Your Line to a Pole

Instead of using your hand-line tackle alone, you can attach it to a pole. You can't cast with a pole that doesn't have a reel, but you can place the bait more accurately.

FINDING THE PERFECT POLE

Your pole should be made of strong wood. It should be stiff but bendable, 5 or 6 feet long, and an inch thick at the bottom narrowing to half an inch at the tip. The first fishing rods were tree branches. A branch from an oak, hickory, hazel, willow, or ash tree is perfect: The wood is soft enough to have a little spring, but hard enough to do the work. It's not a good idea to cut branches from living trees. Find a fallen or recently dead branch, instead. Watch for tree surgeons who are pruning or removing trees in your neighborhood, or search for newly fallen branches after a windy storm. But be careful to avoid rotten, brittle, or cracked wood (see page 58 for ways of testing a rod).

If you find a branch longer than 6 feet, cut off what you don't need. Strip the branch of all smaller twigs and leaves—you want a smooth, straight, flexible pole.

Tie about 6 feet of line to the tip of the pole. Cut a small groove around the tip of the rod so your knot won't slide off.

If you'd rather not make your own pole, you can buy one. Simple 5- or 6-foot bamboo or

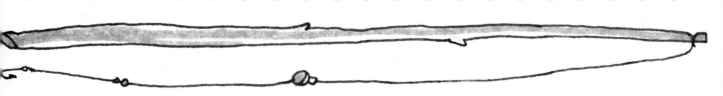

fiberglass poles can be found at discount and sporting goods stores.

A "guide," or "eye," will be attached to the tip of a store-bought pole. Use the anchor knot to attach your line. You'll need a length of line about a foot longer than your pole.

Now you'll be able to drop your bait between water lilies or among the branches of a fallen tree. When you hook a fish, lift up the tip of your rod and pull the rod toward you, hand over hand, until you can grab the line and lead the fish to a landing position. This kind of pole fishing is best for pumpkinseed, bluegill, crappie, and saltwater fish like spot and surfperch, which can be caught from a dock.

Jigging

One of the oldest and easiest ways to fish is "jigging," which is lowering and raising a long line into the water. One of the advantages of jigging is that you cover many depths in the water where fish might be swimming. You can jig with your hand-line, a simple pole, or a rod and reel.

In fresh water and in salt water, from a dock or a boat, with live or artificial bait, jigging is pretty much the same. The idea is to give a little "action" to the bait, to make it move.

Bait your hook, making sure that you have enough weight to help it sink swiftly. The bait must respond to your up-and-down motions; a couple of sinkers attached a foot above the hook should work.

To begin jigging, lower the baited tackle into the water. When it reaches the bottom

TIE THE ANCHOR KNOT

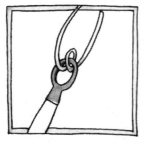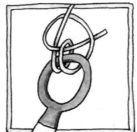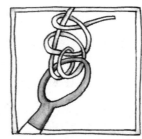

1. Thread your line through the tip's eye two times.

2. Wrap your working end around the line and then feed it through both loops.

3. Wrap your working end around the line one more time, and then feed it through this last loop that you've made.

4. Add a little spit, pull the knot tight, and trim off the extra nylon with fingernail clippers.

(you should feel a "thunk" when the line stops dropping), lift your pole, reel in your line, or pull in your hand-line—whichever you are using. Retrieve your line at a medium speed. When you can see the bait under the surface, lower it again. Raise and lower it, over and over.

Some fish like a slower presentation, so if you have no luck after a few minutes, try jigging slowly for a while. Then try it a little faster.

If your line is very light or the current is strong, you might have a problem getting the bait to jig. In that case use a heavier line just for jigging. You don't need a whole spool, just 7 feet of 8- to 10-pound-test line. The thicker line will respond more swiftly to each raising and lowering.

Lifesaving for Fish

Let's say you're not planning to catch dinner—you're just fishing for the fun of it. Or you catch a fish that is too small to keep, or out of season. How do you treat such a fish so that it will survive? Here are the re-sponsible ways to help a fish survive your catch.

1. Be sure the fish has tired itself before you begin this process. A fish that is still fighting is more likely to be hurt.

2. Keep the fish in the water if you can. (Even if you intend to keep the fish, dangling it in the air is dangerous.) Slide your landing net into the water under the fish until you lift your catch toward you.

3. Wet your hands and hold the fish just behind its head—that is, hold it right over its gill covers. Don't touch its gills or eyes, and don't squeeze its belly. You can keep the fish in the net if that helps you grasp it. All this can be done with the fish under-water.

4. Remove the hook. (With a barbless hook [see page 34], this should be easier.) Don't pull; pulling sinks the hook in deeper. A hook that is sticking through the fish's lip or cheek needs to be backed out. Grab the eye of the hook and try to push it back into the fish's mouth. Once the barbed end is free, you can just slide the hook out of the fish's mouth. Needlenose pliers are often helpful, and with larger game fish like walleye or bluefish that have exposed teeth, pliers are a necessity.

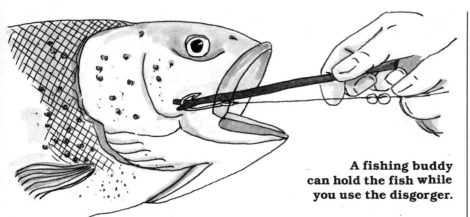

A fishing buddy can hold the fish while you use the disgorger.

If the fish has swallowed the hook, you might need another set of hands. In this case, use a disgorger, a stick with a notch in the end. (This is a handy thing to have in your tackle box.) Slide the stick down the fishing line until it meets the gap of the hook. Then, keeping the line taut, use the stick to dislodge the hook from the fish's throat: Push the stick forward into the throat until the barb is freed. Now slide out the line and the stick together.

If you can't get the hook out quickly, or if it seems you might injure the fish by trying, cut the line close to the hook. The fish's digestive juices will dissolve the hook and the fish will be fine.

5. Help the fish recover. With two wet hands, cradle the fish, one hand under the belly and one hand around the tail. Move the fish back and forth underwater; that will force water into its mouth and out its gills. If you are in a moving stream, turn the fish so that it is facing upstream, "swallowing" the current. The water rushing into its mouth will help the fish breathe. When the fish has recovered, it will begin squirming; let it swim away.

Never "toss a fish back." The impact can damage its inner organs. Even if the fish appears to be fine and swims away from such rough treatment, it will probably die an hour later.

Be sure your hands are wet whenever you touch a fish. Keep a cotton glove in your tackle box, and put it on and

A SLIMY BUT SENSITIVE PROTECTION

The slippery, slimy mucus layer that covers a fish keeps disease and bacteria from harming it.

When you touch a fish you can feel (and, unfortunately, remove) a fish's protective coating. Dry hands will rub off this protection and make the fish vulnerable to bacteria. Sometime you may see or catch a fish that wears a green or brown human handprint on its body. That's the shape of a careless angler's dry hands, and that handprint of bacteria will eventually kill the fish.

wet it before you handle a fish. It will help you hold the fish and keep your hands from removing its protective mucus.

Keeping a Fish for Dinner

As soon as the fish is out of the water, its mucus begins to dry. Bacteria begin to multiply. In just 12 hours, a once fresh, sweet-tasting fish can begin to smell foul and taste spoiled.

So if you've caught a legal fish and you do want to eat it...

1. Kill the fish neatly and quickly to keep it from spoiling or dying slowly. Take a heavy stick or rock and strike the fish on its head, above the eyes. One sharp rap will kill it instantly. (You're likely to fish with someone who uses a stringer—a long rope, often bearing large "safety pins," that are secured through the fish's mouth and gills. The stringer is kept in the water and the fish are killed all at once at the end of the fishing day. But this isn't the best idea for a new angler since it requires more fish handling.)

2. If there is fresh water nearby, rinse or wipe the entire fish.

3. Place the fish on ice in a cooler. If there's no ice, use leaves, ferns, or dampened newspapers to keep the fish cool.

Since blood and internal organs spoil first, some anglers "field dress" their fish. This means they gut the fish before putting it on ice (see page 89).

MAKING A CREEL

Anglers who fish in streams or move up and down the shore while casting need a portable cooler, called a creel.

Make a creel out of an old pillowcase, a burlap or cloth sack (the kind that flour, rice, or grain comes in), or any other fabric bag.

Keep the fish in the bottom of the sack and use the top half for a handle and two lids.

1. Make four cuts a quarter of the way down the sack: two cuts, 2 inches apart; and, directly across the sack, two more cuts, 2 inches apart.

2. Tie or sew the two thin strips (the 2-inch bands) together to create a strap.

3. The two wide flaps can be folded over the day's catch like overlapping lids.

Place your fish inside the creel on top of grass, leaves, or ferns. Add more plants, put another fish on top, and keep going until you've packed up all your fish. Then soak the whole sack in water to keep the fish cool and moist.

FISH, TACKLE, AND BAIT
PART TWO

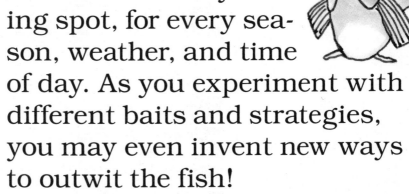

A smart angler asks a question with each cast: What kind of fish will I meet, which tackle will catch that fish, and which bait will be irresistible?

There's a different answer for every kind of fish and every fishing spot, for every season, weather, and time of day. As you experiment with different baits and strategies, you may even invent new ways to outwit the fish!

YOUR TACKLE BOX

The more you fish, the more tackle you're likely to collect. You'll find lost tackle, you'll purchase a few important items, someone will give you an extra lure, or you'll make lures of your own. You'll need a larger tackle box to organize all your small equipment so there won't be tangling, rusting, breakage, or loss.

You can buy a tackle box, or you can find some household object that will work well. It should be lightweight, durable, and made of a material that won't rust.

Here are a few ready-made boxes that might work:

- old plastic sewing box
- art supply box
- plastic lunch box
- men's travel pouch; ladies' cosmetic bag

Since you'll want extra compartments, find other small containers to hold individual pieces of tackle. These holders work well:

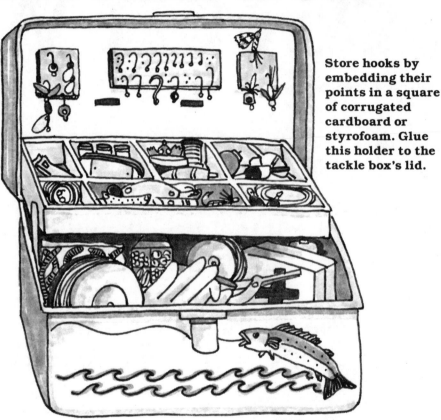

Store hooks by embedding their points in a square of corrugated cardboard or styrofoam. Glue this holder to the tackle box's lid.

- old band-aid tins
- empty prescription bottles
- small plastic jars from kitchen herbs or spices
- paper boxes from cosmetics or jewelry
- plastic canisters that hold camera film
- matchboxes (perfect for protecting that special lure)
- an empty spool or craft stick (wind extra pieces of line around it)

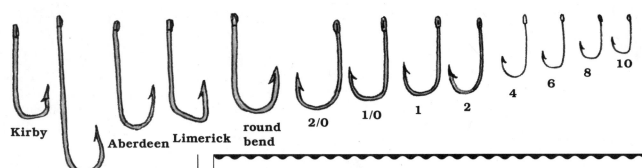

Kirby Carlisle Aberdeen Limerick round bend 2/0 1/0 1 2 4 6 8 10

Hooks

Hooks come in many sizes and shapes. You want a hook that is small enough to slip into a fish's mouth, yet large enough to hold its lip securely. Too large or too small a hook won't "fit" properly, and you'll probably lose the fish.

Hooks are measured with an odd numbering system that

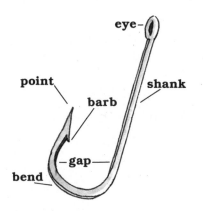

eye

point

barb

shank

gap

bend

HOW TO HANDLE HOOKS

If a hook is sharp enough to pierce the tough lip of fish, it is sharp enough to give you a serious puncture wound. Hooks aren't hard to hold, and they don't jerk from your hands like slippery fish. But accidents can happen. Be careful handling hooks, especially when

➤ removing a hook from a fish's mouth. A fish can twist or flop and expose the hook.

➤ casting or retrieving your line. Don't let a baited hook dangle or swing in the air.

➤ carrying your tackle. Always keep the hook embedded in something. Sink the hand-line or pole hook in a piece of cork or

a soft piece of wood. Keep the hooks in your tackle box stored neatly. And with a rod and reel, slip your hook into one of the guides on your rod and tighten the line to secure the hook in place.

Rusty hooks are particularly dangerous. A rusty hook is weaker and easier to break, and you're much more likely to harm and lose a fish while using a rusty hook. If you come across a rusted hook, wrap it up so that the barb won't accidentally prick someone, and throw it away.

MAKE A BARBLESS HOOK

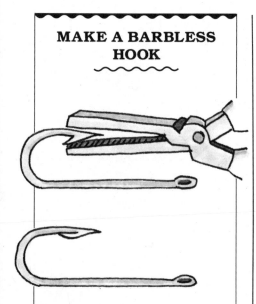

For catch-and-release fishing, a barbless hook makes it easy to unhook a fish. Take any regular hook, and squeeze a pair of pliers over the barb until it bends down and rests against the rest of the hook. The hook should make a simple "J" now, with no extra point. Your hook will snare the fish's lip, but the barb's point won't plant itself a second time inside the fish's lip. Keep your line taut, play the fish right, and you won't need the barb to keep the fish on your hook.

runs from #20 to #0. The bigger the number, the smaller the hook. The numbers aren't printed on hooks, so anglers learn to recognize a hook by sight. Match any hook you happen to have with the chart on page 33 to find its size.

Hooks that are even larger than #0 are used with big game fish. These hooks carry the number 0 from the largest of the smaller hooks and add on another number between 1 and 20 to show that the hook is still bigger. #1/0 is the smallest of these larger hooks, #2/0 is the next largest, and #20/0 is the largest of the series.

A bait hook has a single barb. A snelled hook is a bait hook with a short piece of nylon line attached. A salmon-egg hook has a shorter shank. It is for fishing with corn kernels, marshmallows, and other tiny morsels. A hook with a longer shank makes hook removal easier. It's especially helpful with saltwater fish such as flounder.

There are also hooks with longer shanks, deeper bends, and wider gaps; there are double hooks and triple (treble) hooks. But for our purposes, the basic hook will do quite well if it's clean and sharp.

KEEP HOOKS SHARP

The point of a hook will dull over time (even a new hook isn't always sharp enough). You'll lose a lot of fish if your hook is too dull because it won't penetrate easily, and when it does, it is likely to tear instead of pierce.

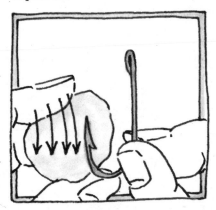

To sharpen a hook, use a metal fingernail file or a smooth stone. Slide the outside of the hook's point down the surface of the sharpener. Four or five downward (not up and down) strokes should do the trick.

Buying hooks can be confusing. It's easy to buy many more than you'll need because hooks are often packaged in multiple sizes. Look for a small pre-packed group of assorted hooks in a size range you'll need.

A Few Lines About Line

Fishing line is rated according to "test." For example, "6-pound-test" means the line has been tested to handle fish up to 6 pounds without breaking. As a beginner, most of the fish you'll be catching will probably weigh less than 6 pounds.

UNCURLING A CURLY LINE
If you keep your line wound around a spool or a stick, it might be curly when you cast it. The coils will keep the line

from extending to its full length and they may absorb the smaller motions of a fish—so you might not feel a strike. To straighten your line, find a small piece of rubber (a piece

TIE THE SURGEON'S KNOT

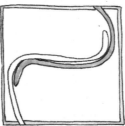 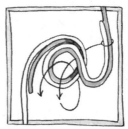 

1. Hold the ends of both lines together, overlapping about 6 inches. Make a simple knot (like the first part of tying shoelaces), holding both strands together.

2. Before tightening the loop, feed both ends of the line through the knot's opening. (You're just adding an extra loop to your overhand knot.)

3. Moisten the knot with spit, and pull tight. Clip off any extra line or string.

TIE THE BLOOD KNOT

 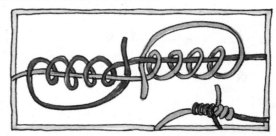

1. Let your two lines overlap about 6 inches. Twist one line four times around the other line, then pass its end through the loop made by the crossing lines.

2. Now twist the other line four times, in the opposite direction, around the first line. Once again, thread the end through the loop.

3. Pull all four ends and close the knot. Add a drop of saliva and tighten completely. Trim off the short ends of both lines.

from a burst inner tube or worn-out galoshes) and tuck it snugly around your pointer finger. Then pull the line across the rubber patch. This will smooth out the kinks.

Inspect your fishing line every so often to make sure it hasn't weakened anywhere along its length. When a fish pulls hard, a line tends to break at the point where there is a knot, twist, fray, or nick.

HANDLING A KNIFE

If your parent or guardian will give you permission to keep a small Boy Scout or Swiss Army knife in your tackle box, it will come in handy cutting line, opening split-shot sinkers, slicing large bait into smaller pieces, and many other ways. Always cut away from your hands. Use the palm of your hand to close the blade, keeping your other fingers away from its slot. Keep your blade clean, sharp, and dry. One or two small blades is plenty. You won't need a blade longer than 3 inches.

BUYING NEW LINE

Buying line at a tackle shop can be bewildering and expensive. There is clear, blue, yellow, green, brown, and even "chameleon" line. Spools of line have different "tests" or strengths.

Buy the best line you can afford. Cheap line tends to be weak, breakable, curly, or uneven in strength.

Beginners often prefer a colored line—it's easier to see the twitches and movements of a colored line.

Buy monofilament line—that is, a line with one strand. There are braided lines, too, but you can pass these up for now.

As for strength, keep using 4- to 6-pound-test line; it will give you a line that responds quickly to a fish's strike and is unlikely to break. If you are fishing in water full of rocks and stumps or for heavier fish, you might want a heavier line—say, 10-pound-test. The line will be more resistant to scuffing and scraping. For fishing in streams with some of the lures you may make, you might want a 2- to 4-pound-test line; this lighter line will allow the lures to travel along with the current more naturally, rising and falling under the surface.

FISHING WITH KITE STRING

In a pinch, you can fish with kite string, but first color the line blue or green with a crayon. Tie a length of kite string between two trees to keep the line taut, then run your crayon up and down the line until it is colored and waterproofed.

Leave your new coated line in the sun for a few hours so that the wax melts into the fibers.

Fish might still be spooked by the colored string. To make your line more invisible to them, tie 2 feet of nylon line at one end of your string using a surgeon's knot (see page 35). This added line is called a leader. A clear leader attached to any line will help convince the fish that your bait is a safe snack.

TIE A WEIGHTED LEADER

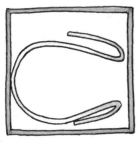

1. Take about 2 feet of fishing line.

2. Tie one surgeon's knot at each end to make a small, permanent loop.

3. Don't forget to trim off any extra line.

4. On one end, attach your plummet. Slide the loop all the way through the eye of the plummet, and then pull it over the end of the plummet. Attach your hook to the other end of the line in the same way.

5. You now have a double leader that's about 20 inches long. Attach your fishing line to this leader with a blood knot.

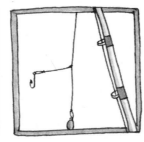

6. Place your line 8 inches from the plummet and about 12 inches from your hook.

A Weighty Subject

Sinkers add the needed weight to carry your bait to the fish—across the surface and down toward the bottom. You need the least amount of weight that will do the job. An overweighted line snags in weeds or buries itself in mud, presents a bait that is too heavy and unnatural to the fish, and prevents you from feeling a fish's nibbling or strike.

If you need to buy more weight, #7 split-shot sinkers are a good purchase since you can add them together to make a heavier line.

To remove split shot from a line, use a knife. (A dull blade works best for this.) Carefully insert the blade into the seam clamped on the line. Twist the knife slightly to pry apart the halves of the sinkers.

Some sinkers have a forked tail; this makes it easy to remove the weight from the line: Squeeze the tail with pliers to release the line from the grip of the sinker.

The plummet sinker can help you determine the water's depth (see page 21), and it can be used to keep your bait near the

WARNING

LEAD IS POISONOUS

Water birds like ducks and swans need gravel in their gizzards to digest food. An angler's lost sinkers look just like pebbles to a bird and are often swallowed by mistake. Once inside the bird, the lead dissolves and causes a slow and painful death. Be extra careful not to lose lead tackle.

In America, the majority of lead found in the digestive tracts of birds comes from the guns of waterfowl hunters—6 million pounds every year.

The lead from anglers' tackle, however, does contribute to the problem. In England, it is now illegal for anglers to use lead sinkers. By 1987, when their law was passed, 3,000 English swans were dying every year from lead poisoning. Today British anglers fish with weights forged from other metals, such as tungsten and steel.

In the United States, anglers don't have such a law to follow—at least for now.

bottom in moving water, which tends to make bait rise. When fishing from a moving boat or in water with a lot of current, tie a weighted leader (see page 37).

A QUICK WAY TO GAIN WEIGHT

Corked bottles of wine are sealed with lead wrappers. Ask an adult to save you these flat, bendable pieces of lead. You can easily tear a short strip

of the lead and add it to your line for a quick bit of weight. Stream-fishing anglers often carry these lead strips in a pocket to weight their drifting lines.

FRESHWATER FISH

In a small pond, lake, creek, quarry, or reservoir, you're likely to catch these kinds of fish.

The Sunfish Family

Sunfish are flat rather than fat, and on the small side—usually from 4 to 10 inches. They have spiny dorsal fins, small mouths, and a wide variety of bright colors.

BLUEGILL

Anglers catch lots of bluegills in early spring, pole fishing from a dock, or wading in shallow water.

PUMPKINSEED

The most common and wide-spread of the sunfish, the pumpkinseed is found nearly everywhere from May until October.

The pumpkinseed likes warm, weedy waters where there is plentiful food and lots of hiding places. Because they reproduce so successfully, these fish often exhaust their food supply. This means that adult pumpkinseeds may never reach

BLUEGILL
Average size: 6 to 7 inches; 3 to 6 ounces
You can identify a bluegill by its two dark spots on each side: one on the small bump of each gill cover, and another at the end of its dorsal fin. Its pectoral fin is long and pointed; vertical bars line its sides and back.

PUMPKINSEED
Average size: 4 to 7 inches; 3 to 5 ounces
No other freshwater fish is so dazzlingly colored: a greenish back, blue-and-orange sides, a bright red spot on its gill cover, and a softer, dotted dorsal fin.

their full size.

Strategy: Use your basic rig: split-shot sinker, #6 hook, bobber, and monofilament line. Bait the hook with small worms, nymphs, grasshoppers, or crickets. A hand-line dropped from a dock, a pole with a short line, or a simple rod and reel will do the job.

Good baits for sunfish in early spring would be smaller worms: grubworms and red worms or cut-up nightcrawlers. If you are jigging from a dock or reeling in from the bank, do it slowly.

CRAPPIE

Anglers fish for crappie (pronounced CROP-ee) throughout the nation, especially in early spring.

Strategy: Cast with a spinning rod or use a pole from a shady bank. Bait your hook with small minnows (their favorites), worms, or lures such as a small bug, plug, or jig. (For catching, baiting, and storing minnows, see page 48.)

LARGEMOUTH BASS

Found in all states but Alaska, these fish prefer shallower water with lots of places to hide. Identify the largemouth by its greenish back that becomes light green on its sides.

Strategy: Minnows and nightcrawlers are good bait for these nibblers. Make sure your bait is firmly attached to your hook. Cast the bait near their hiding places—weeds, sunken logs, lily pads, and stumps—and allow the bass to strike. Mornings and evenings are the preferred mealtimes.

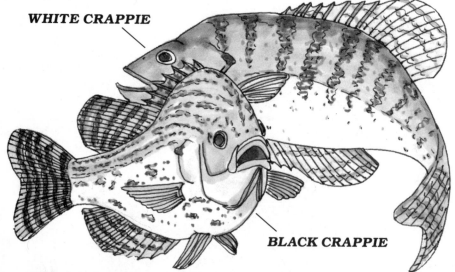

WHITE CRAPPIE

BLACK CRAPPIE

Average size: 6 to 12 inches; ½ to 1 pound.
The white crappie has dark markings that form small bands on its back. Its body is more stretched out than the black crappie, which has a rounder body shape.

THINKING OF A SUNFISH DINNER?

If you are hoping for a dinner of sunfish, be ready to work. While their flesh is sweet and tasty, they'll need to be scaled, gutted, and filleted before cooking. That's slow-going work—and most people will eat several fish. If you're not up for this job, catch sunfish on barbless hooks and follow the steps for carefully releasing fish.

SMALLMOUTH BASS

Smallmouth bass are a good match for anglers. They are wary and difficult to please and, for their size, good fighters. Smallmouths love clear and unpolluted water that isn't too hot or too cold, and a rocky shoreline with lots of weedy cover. They are found in northern and eastern rivers and lakes, and in southern Canada.

Strategy: In early spring, use your bobber to suspend a minnow above a likely bass

spot. By late spring, when the water has warmed, use crayfish; in summer, smallmouths will prefer a meal of crickets to almost anything. You can also try small plugs and spoons.

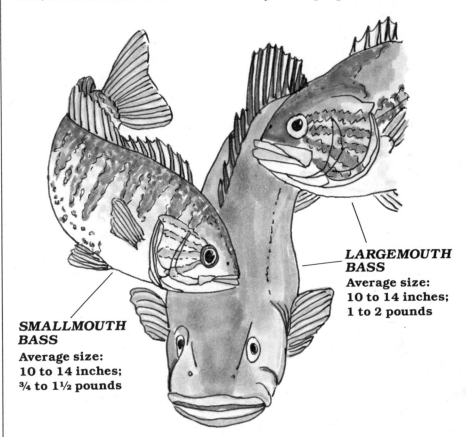

SMALLMOUTH BASS
Average size:
10 to 14 inches;
¾ to 1½ pounds

LARGEMOUTH BASS
Average size:
10 to 14 inches;
1 to 2 pounds

EASY DOES IT IN THE SPRING

In winter, a fish rests in deeper water, living off its stored fat. Its usual functions—eating, breathing, and moving—almost stop.

Even in the warmer waters of March and April, fish are still slow-moving and hesitant, so anglers use smaller bait and slower presentation. The fish aren't ready for large meals and energetic chases.

LARGE- OR SMALLMOUTH BASS?

Look for a blotchy vertical striping all along the body of a smallmouth bass. The largemouth will have only one long, lateral stripe from gill to tail. Then look at the fish's jaw, at the square end of the fish's top lip. If that jaw doesn't extend beyond its eye, you've got a smallmouth bass. And last, a smallmouth bass won't have a deep notch in its dorsal fin; the largemouth will have a spiny dorsal fin and then a separate, flexible second lobe.

Perch Family

YELLOW PERCH

Perch travel in large shoals through clean, slow rivers and wide, open ponds. If you catch one perch, you're likely to catch more. Perch are widespread in the Great Lakes states and areas east of the Mississippi, from Maine to the Florida panhandle. There are also many varieties of saltwater perch (see page 86).

Strategy: Anglers fish for perch all year long. Use a handline, pole, or rod and reel. Bait choices include minnows, worms, and nymphs; or try tiny spoons, plugs, and jigs.

WALLEYE

East of the Mississippi River, a favorite member of the perch family is the walleye, which frequently grows to 15 pounds.

Strategy: Walleyes will bite on minnows, especially in the spring. In warmer summer waters, nightcrawlers are a good choice. Walleyes usually feed in shoals at the bottom of a lake. Use a large #1/0 hook and split-shot sinkers for weight.

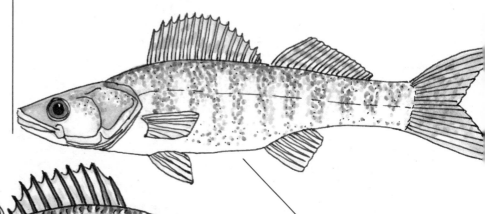

WALLEYE
Average size: 12 to 20 inches; 1 to 3 pounds

A walleye is a long, steel-gray fish with an olive-green back and two special markings: white tips on its tail and anal fin; and a dorsal fin divided into two blades. One identifying trait you don't want to discover: teeth that are sharp enough to teach a careless angler a good lesson. Use a glove or needle-nose pliers when removing a hook from a walleye's mouth.

YELLOW PERCH
Average size: 6 to 8 inches; 2 to 6 ounces

The bright yellow sides of a perch are unmistakable. You'll also find six to eight blackish bars along the perch's side, a generally olive-green body, and a notch dividing its dorsal fin in two.

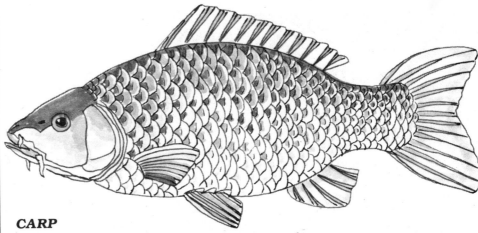

CARP
Average size: 12 to 20 inches; 1 to 10 pounds

A carp is a broad, big fish with large, overlapping scales. Its body is an olive-green that fades to a yellowish belly. The bottom half of the caudal and anal fins are usually reddish. You'll also notice two small barbels around the carp's lips, and a toothless mouth.

Carp Family

CARP

The goldfish in an aquarium is a carp. Can you imagine a 50-pound carp as a pet? It's true, the common goldfish and the carp are close relatives. Carp were brought to Europe from Asia in the Middle Ages, and then shipped to North America about a hundred years ago. In that little time, the carp has made its home throughout most of this continent, particularly the eastern half. In fact, the carp has bred so heavily, it has harmed the natural balance of some native fish and plants. Biologists and anglers have had to work hard to keep this fish in check.

Strategy: The carp is a bottom feeder that enjoys a wide range of odd tidbits such as doughball, corn, nightcrawlers, bread, and potatoes. Use any of your rigs and cast from the shore. Look for spots of churned up, cloudy water—they often signal a carp's presence.

Catfish Family

There are fifteen families of catfish around the world, and you're likely to encounter several species nearly anywhere in the United States: The yellow, brown, or black bullhead, the channel catfish, and even the larger flathead catfish.

Strategy: Ideal catfish baits include nightcrawlers, dead minnows, giant grasshoppers, and bits of chicken entrails (the cut-up organs often stuffed inside a whole packaged chicken).

WARNING

DON'T TOUCH

The dorsal or pectoral spines on the fins of a catfish are not only sharp but they also contain an irritant that will bruise your hands. Use gloves when removing a hook from a catfish, and keep your hands away from the spines.

Your basic rig (split-shot sinker, #6 hook, 4- to 6-pound-test line) is the perfect setup. Prop your pole or rod on a forked stick and wait for the catfish to inhale your tasty offering. Even after rains and in cloudy water, catfish are feeding, using their barbels to scavenge along the bottom.

Trout Family

TROUT
For many anglers, the wonderful taste of these fish is less motivation than how beautiful, feisty, and clever they can be. These trout are especially plentiful in the Great Lakes, Pacific Coast waters, and the streams of Western states.

Strategy: Minnows, worms, and grasshoppers are fine live baits for trout, but anglers think

Lake Trout

Brook Trout

Rainbow Trout

CHANNEL CATFISH

Average size: 10 to 20 inches; 1 to 5 pounds

All catfish have barbels around the mouth and a smooth, scaleless body. Their dorsal fins are compact and round.

BULLHEAD CATFISH

Average size: 8 to 10 inches; 4 to 8 ounces

of trout as the perfect fish for artificial flies. If you know anglers who really love trout, see if they'll take you fly-fishing.

Brown Trout

A rainbow trout has a broad red or pink band along its side, and dark spots along its silvery blue head, back, and tail. The brown trout has yellow or orange spots surrounded by light halos. The brook trout has small red spots along its side, and squiggled markings along its back. The lake trout is less brilliantly colored, wider, and mottled over its whole body with whiter spots.

RECORD WEIGHTS FOR FRESHWATER FISH

All anglers dream of bringing in The Big Fish, a fish that breaks all records, or at least a personal record. Here are the record weights for fish caught in North America:

Largemouth bass 1932
Wt: 22 pounds 4 ounces
Montgomery Lake, GA

Smallmouth bass 1955
Wt: 11 pounds 15 ounces
Dale Hollow Lake, KY

White bass 1979
Wt: 5 pounds 6 ounces
Grenada, MS

Bluegill 1950
Wt: 4 pounds 12 ounces
Ketona Lake, AL

Bullhead 1951
Wt: 8 pounds
Lake Waccabuc, NY

Carp 1952
Wt: 55 pounds 5 ounces
Clearwater Lake, MN

Channel catfish 1964
Wt: 58 pounds
Santee-Cooper Reservoir, SC

White crappie 1957
Wt: 5 pounds 3 ounces
Enid Dam, MS

Muskelunge 1957
Wt: 69 pounds 15 ounces
St. Lawrence River, NY

Yellow perch 1865
Wt: 4 pounds 3 ounces
Bordentown, NJ

Brook trout 1916
Wt: 14 pounds 8 ounces
Nipigon River, Ont., Canada

Rainbow trout 1970
Wt: 42 pounds 2 ounces
Bell Island, AK

Walleye 1960
Wt: 25 pounds
Old Hickory Lake, TN

Is it just a coincidence that most of these fishing records haven't been broken in more than twenty—or even forty—years? Most experts think this says something about the poorer quality of the fish's environment.

BAITING UP

There are several kinds of bait. Natural baits are live things a fish can usually find in its environment: flies, larvae, nymphs, smaller fish, plants. Cut baits are part of a larger creature that a fish might be tempted to eat: pieces of a squid, a crab, or a night-crawler, or strips of bait fish. Artificial baits are the plastic, metal, or rubber lures you hope the fish will mistake for its real food.

Fishy Tidbits

Here are some unusual baits no fish is likely to find in its waters unless an angler is nearby. Try them. They work! No doubt you'll come up with lots of other crazy baits if you check with anglers in your area.

Bread. Squash and form the bread into a ball around your hook. Catfish, carp, and other grazing fish can't resist, especially if you mix in a little juice from a tin of tuna fish, sardines, or cat food.

DOUGHBALL: A FISH'S FAVORITE RECIPE

Every angler and bait store probably has a recipe for doughball, a bait that carp and catfish particularly like. Here's an easy version that makes enough doughball to feed a whole school of fish!

Mix together with your hands:

- 1 cup flour
- 3 or 4 tablespoons bacon drippings or cod-liver oil
- 1 tablespoon water

The dough should be very smooth, heavy, and stiff. Try rolling a small piece into a neat ball. If the ball holds together, it will stay on your hook. If it doesn't, add more water, a teaspoon at a time. Adding a few shreds of a cotton ball will help the dough-ball stay on the hook.

And now for the angler's secret: add a few drops of flavoring. Anise extract and banana extract seem to be fish favorites.

Store doughball in an air-tight plastic bag and use it within a week or so. Freeze any extra; just remember to thaw it a few hours before you go fishing.

Sweet corn. A salmon-egg hook threaded with kernels of canned corn is great for carp.

Candy. Carp have a sweet tooth, too. They like gum drops, jelly beans, and marshmallows.

Cheese. A little dab of a firm cheese like Swiss or Jack covering a hook will attract perch, carp, catfish, and sunfish. Use the strongest-smelling cheese that's handy—the fish will sniff it out better.

Meats. Leftover meats, hot dogs, and lunch meats are gourmet items for sunfish, catfish, carp, chub, and even a few predator fish.

Chicken necks. Blue crabs love these. You don't even need a hook. Just tie a neck on a line and start jigging from the dock. When you pull up your line, the crab will be holding the neck in one of its powerful claws.

Potatoes, carrots, pasta shapes, chick peas, and shelled peanuts. Cook until barely soft but not mushy. Prebait—that is, give away free samples for a couple of nights so that the fish acquire a taste for this new, unusual food.

TWO QUICK CRICKET TRAPS

You can buy crickets at the bait store, but why not catch them yourself? You'll have to stay up a little late to set the first trap. Before sundown, place small handfuls of cornmeal by a woodpile, on the ground next to your house's foundation, or

on the sidewalk or driveway bordering the lawn. Every 30 minutes after sundown, return to the spot with a flashlight and your minnow net. Shine your light on the piles, drop your net over the cornmeal, and pluck up your crickets. Store them in a jar with holes punched in the lid.

If you can't stay up catching crickets, make this great cricket trap. Take a loaf of day-old—or even older!—unsliced bread. Cut the loaf in half lengthwise and scoop out most of the soft bread inside. At the end of one half, cut out a half-dollar-size hole. Put the halves back together and join them with string or rubber bands. If there's a field with high grass nearby, set your trap there.

In the morning, retrieve your trap and shake the crickets into your jar.

MAKE A MINNOW TRAP

Staple a piece of cheese-cloth (available at any grocery or hardware store) on two long wooden sticks. Make a kind of hammock or valley in the fabric, so that it sinks in the center. Then simply set your trap near a group of minnows, toss your crumbs over the sunken cloth, wait until the minnows swim over, and then lift the two sticks up and together. Quickly scoop the minnows into a bucket.

A Cricket for a Smallmouth

One thing a smallmouth bass loves is a cricket. Crickets are mid- to late-summer creatures. Fish with them especially when smallmouths are surface feeding (you can often spot them with non-glare sunglasses).

Strategy: Use a small hook, even a #8, since a cricket is a small morsel. Hook the cricket by its collar: Insert the hook behind the head and lift it back up on the body side.

Minnows

Redfins, shad, shiners, chubs—minnows come in many shapes and sizes and they are the favorite foods of many fish. The minnow is a good bet for bass, crappie, striper, pike, walleye, and catfish. Saltwater varieties are perfect for flounder, small bluefish, and rock bass.

If you store your minnows in a bucket, keep the water out of the sun and change the water as soon as they start breathing at the surface; they'll use up the oxygen very quickly.

Use your fishing net to gather your own minnows if the mesh is small enough. Set the net in the water near a group of minnows. Toss bread crumbs over the net and wait until the minnows are within the net's rim. Then lift the net quickly and drop the captured minnows into your minnow bucket or holder. If your net's mesh is too big, you can make a minnow trap.

You can also keep your minnows underwater in a perforated or mesh bucket. You can make your own flow-through minnow bucket from a plastic bucket, a large margarine tub, or any other plastic container with a lid.

When fishing a stream, hook the lips so that the minnow looks as if it's swimming naturally.

When fishing a lake or pond, hook the minnow just under the dorsal fin.

RODS, REELS, AND OTHER RIGS
PART THREE

Now you're ready for a day of fishing. Learn to judge the weather and the time of day to know when the fish are biting. Find the prime lies, the places in a pond or stream where fish gather. Bring along a fishing buddy.

With a rod and reel, you'll cast farther and deeper into the water. You'll try artificial baits such as spinners, plugs, and spoons. There are plenty of fishing tricks yet to learn, and soon you'll have your own supply of sure-fire lures and angling secrets.

A DAY OF FISHING

Fishing is ideal early (March, April, May) and late (September, October) in the fishing season, when the water temperature is not too cold or too warm. Too early in the year or too late in the year, the fish will be sluggish and hesitant to strike. When you're sweating through those hot August days, the fish, like you, would rather stay cool. Lake fish head away from the shoreline. They look for deeper, colder holes, cool springs, or the mouth of a cold stream that feeds the lake. Stream fish rush for the base of rapids or waterfalls—the water there is cooler and mixed with lots of oxygen.

Early morning and early evening are the best times for fishing—that's when the fish are usually feeding.

In southern states, the fishing season lasts most of the year since the water temperature doesn't change as much as it does in more northern regions.

In larger bodies of water, such as an ocean bay or wide river, temperatures don't change as rapidly as they do in small ponds or streams. The water flows so quickly that a few hot days won't affect the fish's place in the water. Still, try early morning or evening fishing.

At the ocean, time your fishing with the tides. Incoming tides bring in the food. Outgoing tides do not. So the best fishing is two hours before and two hours after high tide— that's when the incoming tide has brought all the water and food closer to shore. One hour before dawn is also a good time, when the sun has yet to warm the surface.

Weather-Wise Fishing

A smart angler weighs many factors before venturing out for a day of fishing. Whether or not you'll be able to catch fish may

CHECKLIST FOR A DAY OF FISHING

For a successful day of fishing, you'll need a few more things than a stocked tacklebox, hand-line or rod, and bait. Use this checklist to decide what you need before you set off for the day.

☐ a sunscreen with a high SPF (sun protection factor)

☐ a hat or cap

☐ insect repellent

☐ long pants and socks (if you'll be walking through fields)

☐ old shoes you won't mind getting wet or muddy (with traction, if you might be fishing from a slippery dock or boat)

☐ lunch or a snack (keep it in your cooler)

☐ creel or cooler (if you are planning to eat your catch)

☐ minnow net (if you need to catch minnows)

☐ minnow bucket (if you need to store minnows)

☐ cloth gloves for handling and releasing fish

☐ snake-bite kit (if there are dangerous snakes in your area)

☐ life jacket (if you are fishing from a boat or near deep water or if you are still learning to swim)

☐ sunglasses (yellow, polarized)

☐ a landing net

☐ a camera or a sketchbook for a quick "capturing" of your fish

☐ a tape measure for a quick measuring

☐ a portable radio (with headphones)

☐ a poncho or raincoat (if a storm is brewing)

☐ a pocket knife (along with an adult's permission)

depend on the weather conditions.

The chief rule is: nice day, nice fishing. If it's not too hot or cold, too cloudy or windy, too hazy or humid, you've found favorable conditions.

COUNT THE CHIRPS

For the current temperature, listen to the "Crickets' Broadcasting Frequency." It is always reporting the temperature. Look at your wristwatch. Now count how many chirps a nearby cricket makes in 15 seconds. Add 37. That's the temperature in degrees Fahrenheit. (For example: 40 chirps in 15 seconds means it's 77 degrees outside.)

NATURE'S FORECAST. RAIN IS JUST AHEAD WHEN...

... spiders crawl out onto their webs
... bees leave the fields and return to their hives
... trees "fold up" or cup their leaves
... birds perch in trees and along telephone wires
... cows lie down in the fields

IT'S RAINING CATS AND DOGS AND FISH!

Catfish, carp, and many other fish feed like crazy during a rain. It's probably because the rain washes insects from the air and other foods from the shore into the water. Some anglers like fishing in the rain. If you have the rain gear and the interest, you might try fishing during rain.

Warning: Rain, that is, not a heavy downpour or a storm with lightning. *Never* stay in or on the water during a storm. When thunder is near, go directly to shore. Bodies of water are often struck by lightning.

Right after a rain is also a good time for fishing, but be extra careful walking along a slippery dock or muddy bank. Use your most brightly colored fishing line; it will help you see into the murkier water.

Prime Lies

Where do fish congregate in a body of water? The likeliest places are called prime lies— the prime places for catching fish. Most fish look for several things in the water, and if you look for the same things, you'll find your fish.

at the base of a rocky cliff

at the mouth of an incoming creek

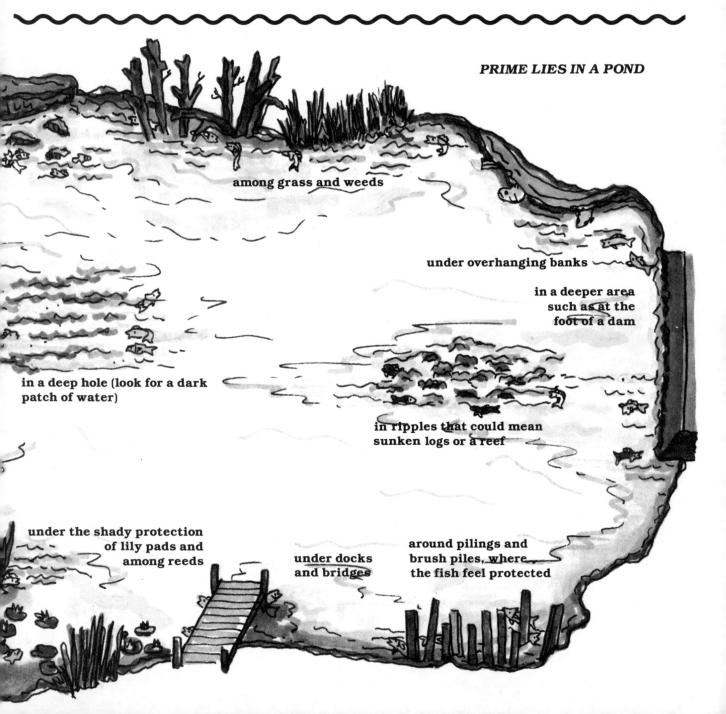

PRIME LIES IN A POND

among grass and weeds

under overhanging banks

in a deeper area
such as at the
foot of a dam

in a deep hole (look for a dark
patch of water)

in ripples that could mean
sunken logs or a reef

under the shady protection
of lily pads and
among reeds

under docks
and bridges

around pilings and
brush piles, where
the fish feel protected

A fish needs:

🐟 a place to hide from predators

🐟 a place to look for food

🐟 a place with enough oxygen

🐟 a place to rest in the current

For instance, a boulder in the middle of the stream would soften the current's flow, offer a fish a sense of shelter, and bring all kinds of appetizing foods right past the fish. Instead of tossing your line just any old place where there's water, look for prime lies.

FACING UP TO STREAM FISH

Remember that the stream fish hiding in these lies will be facing upstream, into the current. Cautious anglers try to use the fish's blind spot—directly behind it—and walk undetected against the current as it flows downstream.

TROUTS AND WORMS

If you are using a worm and bottom-fishing for trout, be certain you have enough split-shot sinkers on the line to keep the worm down amid the rush-ing current. When your trout does bite, give it a chance to take the whole worm; then set the hook firmly.

Angling Advice

When fishing around other anglers, notice what kind of tackle they are using. Don't be afraid to ask questions. Most anglers are eager to offer tips, share advice, spread the good luck. They might have an idea of where another prime lie

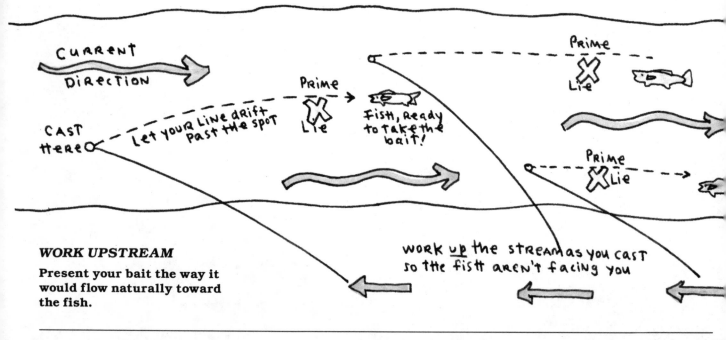

CURRENT DIRECTION

PRIME Lie

FISH, Ready to take the bait!

CAST HERE

Let your line drift past the spot

PRIME Lie

PRIME Lie

WORK UPSTREAM

Present your bait the way it would flow naturally toward the fish.

work up the stream as you cast so the fish aren't facing you might be, what fish are biting, which kind of lure or bait to use.

At a tackle shop, ask the person behind the counter or someone shopping there: "Do you know of a nearby fishing spot for bass?" or "I'm going fishing for crappie. What do they seem to be biting on this week?"

Anglers are off by themselves a lot of the time, keeping quiet and being patient, so they've built up a lot of unused social time. Many are happy to talk and give advice to interested fellow anglers.

BE A COURTEOUS ANGLER

Though you should talk to and watch other anglers, remember that every angler deserves to fish without interference or too many interruptions. The first to arrive should be respected by later anglers. In a stream, especially, recently arriving anglers should fish downstream of the established anglers, to avoid taking away fish the earlier anglers will meet working up the stream. Arriving at a pond, pick a place far enough away from the other anglers so that your lines won't cross and your conversation won't be heard.

HOW LONG UNTIL DARK?

You've found the perfect fishing hole, the fish are almost jumping onto your hook—but the sun is sinking and you want to be home before dark. Estimate the remaining daylight this way: Raise your arm (don't bend your elbow) and cover the sun with the back of your hand. You should be looking at the flat palm of your hand. Now lower your hand. How many fingers can you fit between the sun and the horizon line? Each finger that fits means 15 minutes of sun— that is, 15 more minutes of fishing, or 15 minutes to pack your gear and dash home!

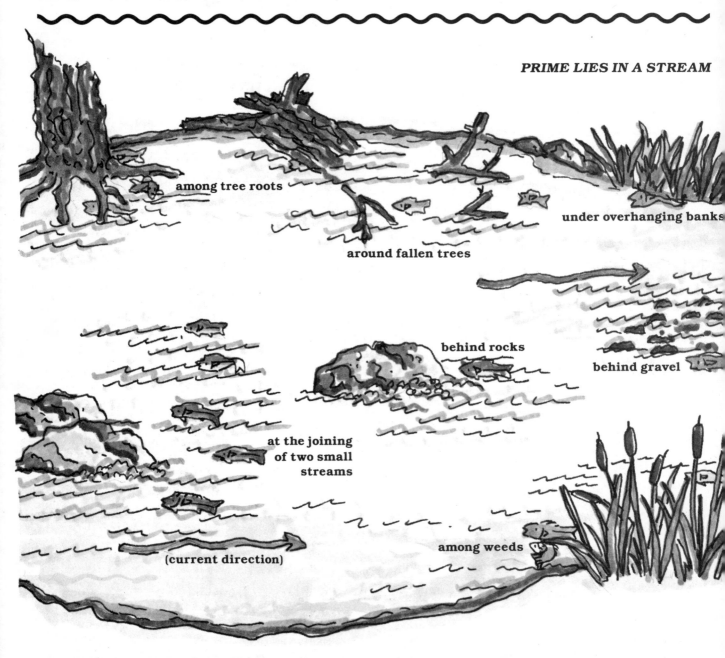

PRIME LIES IN A STREAM

among tree roots

under overhanging banks

around fallen trees

behind rocks

behind gravel

at the joining
of two small
streams

among weeds

(current direction)

THE INVISIBLE TACKLE BOX

You may have wonderful equipment, a well-stocked tackle box, a perfect fishing hole, and just the right bait—but not even a nibble! Probably the fish just aren't biting where you are today. All you can do is move on, try again later, or just enjoy the beautiful afternoon.

But perhaps the fish aren't biting because you've forgotten your other tackle box, the one that you carry in your head and your fingers and your five senses.

This is the tackle box of experience. And with fishing, experience counts. In this invisible tackle box, you store:

Everything you're learning about how fish behave, what fish bite on, where fish hide. That's material you're always gathering. Like invisible lures, each fact that you learn will help you nab a great catch.

Curiosity. Most anglers are constantly wondering

how and why and what if. The lure that was sure-fire yesterday is a dud today. The fish were here last week; where did they go? Locating, attracting, and hooking fish is a puzzle that an angler tries to solve each time a cast is

made. Be sure your invisible tackle box has a place for unsolved mysteries, unanswered questions, and good guesses.

Your five senses and a good memory bank. These are invisible, too, but you rely

on their information each time you fish. The sounds and colors of the water, the air and water temperature, the clouds overhead, the direction of the current and depth of your bait—a good angler's senses grasp all those details.

Good advice. Your invisible tackle box can store all kinds of angling news: weather forecasts, newspaper columns, bait store advice, books you've read, and suggestions from other anglers.

A big spool of patience. Some days you need to loosen the drag and let out a lot of patience. Patience can be more attractive to fish than a fancy lure.

Determination. You need a full compartment of determination just to keep you from giving up.

Luck. Some days it's just plain luck that counts; anglers always have a little of this going for them.

ROD AND REEL FISHING

Fishing with a rod and reel will give you a chance to reach fish that are deeper and farther from shore. You'll have a better chance at casting long distances and catching many kinds of fish.

Buying a Rod and Reel

Most hardware, discount, and sporting goods stores have rod-and-reel sets made for younger anglers. These sets are sized to be more comfortable, and are often priced to be affordable. This will be an important purchase, so be sure to ask a more experienced fishing buddy to help with your selection.

In general, a fiberglass rod is less expensive, and a 5- or 6-foot rod will feel most comfortable. This checklist will help you select the best rod for you.

Feel. Find a rod that feels comfortable in your hand.

Flexibility. You want a rod with good flexibility in the tip, and more stiffness farther down the pole. To test your rod, hold its handle and shake your hand up and down, whipping the tip up and down. You don't want a flimsy rod that bends all the way down its length. And you don't want a rigid rod that only bends at the very tip. Try several rods.

Looks. If it's a tie between two rods, pick the color and shape and design you like best.

Price. Choose the best rod that you can afford. A rod made of good materials with fine workmanship is more likely to last without breaking, splintering, rusting or losing its hardware.

The Reel Question

Like rods, there are many kinds of reels with many different uses. If you buy a rod-and-reel set, the manufacturer has already matched the right rod with the right reel.

CLOSED-FACE OR OPEN-FACE?

There are two kinds of spinning reels. The closed-face spinning reel is trouble-free, inexpensive, and easy to use. The line is sealed inside a covered case that rests on top of the rod. A simple button, worked by your thumb, releases the line.

In the open-face reel, you can see the spool of line; it hangs underneath the rod. There's no cover and no button;

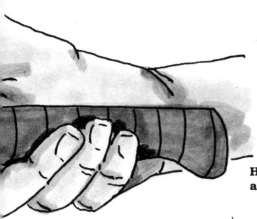

Holding a closed-face reel (left) and an open-face reel (above).

instead, there is a curving bar, called a bail, that regulates the line leaving and entering the reel. It's easier to change spools of fishing line with an open-face reel.

CASTING WITH A CLOSED-FACE REEL

First make sure the reel is in place and the line is threaded through the guides (metal rings). The reel should be tightly screwed into its slot on the rod, and the line (which you can release by pressing the button) should run straight through each of the rod's guides without circling or tangling.

Tie your plummet to the end of the line. Leave about 6 inches of the line hanging from the rod's tip. Reel in any extra line—always wind in a forward direction.

Now find a wide-open clearing. Hold the rod in your right hand (unless you're left-handed), and point the tip of the rod just above your target.

If your rod has a special grip for your first finger, hook it in place. Rest your thumb on the casting button. Now raise your arm, bending at the elbow, until the tip of the rod just passes your ear and points directly behind you.

You're now ready to perform an overhead cast. Push the button with your thumb and keep it held down. Now whip the rod forward and release the button at the same time. Start that motion with your wrist, then follow with your forearm until you are pointing almost

OVERHEAD CAST

1. Keep your thumb on the button.

2. Bend your elbow and point the rod behind you. Push the button.

3. Release the button as you whip the rod forward.

SIDEARM CAST

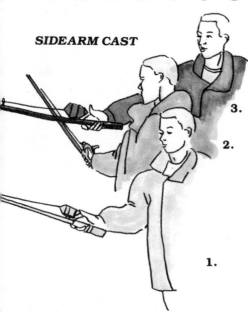

3.

2.

1.

Swing your arm to the side instead of over your shoulder.

straight ahead—not quite even with the ground. The weight should send your line straight ahead of you.

Did the line hit the ground right in front of you? You didn't release the button soon enough.

Did the line fly high into the air above you? You released the button too soon.

Practice until you can land the weight right where you want it—near to or far from, left of or right of, behind or in front of an obstacle.

If you are fishing below the limbs of overhanging trees, use the sidearm cast. It offers you a lower cast that won't get tangled in branches.

CASTING WITH AN OPEN-FACE REEL

Once again, make sure your rod is ready for casting. Your reel should be secured underneath the rod, and the line should run straight through all the rod's guides. Now attach your plummet weight, and make sure nothing stands in the way of your casting.

Grip the rod comfortably with your right hand (unless you are a lefty). Most anglers put two fingers in front of the reel post (the bar that holds the reel in place) and two fingers in back of the post. Secure the fishing line with your first finger and press it firmly against the rod. With your free left hand, swing the bail to the other side until it holds in its open position and releases line.

The cast itself is the same that as with a closed-face reel.

Once your cast has landed, you'll reel in the slack line, and the bail will swing back to its closed position, preventing more line from slipping out.

ADDING NEW LINE

You'll need to add new line if your reel doesn't come with line, if your old line is nicking and wearing out, or if you want to fish with line of a different weight.

To attach new line, tie one end in a double knot around the spool of your reel.

Now wind the line onto the spool, holding the entering line with two fingers so that it wraps

Your finger holds the line against the rod while it moves to the cocked position behind your head.

1.

tightly. Most spools will have a small bar that helps the line distribute itself evenly over the spool. If yours does not, you'll need to guide your line so that it weaves back and forth across the spool, covering its whole width. Keep up this back and forth motion until the spool is filled.

Your first finger will help keep the line from running out; the drag will help, too.

Your Direct Line to the Fish

The bobber isn't the only way to detect a fish. If you are pole or rod-and-reel fishing, watch the tip of your rod. Most of the time it should be straight, bending only slightly as current tugs the line. But if the tip bends down suddenly, that can only mean one thing: Something wants your bait! Usually

When the wrist begins its forward swing, the finger lifts off the line.

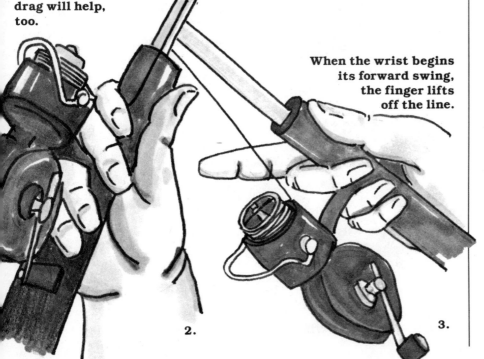

2.

3.

SETTING THE DRAG

Drag is how much your reel "holds on to the line"—its "grip." Your reel should let a strong fish draw out line so that it doesn't break—but the line should resist enough so that the fish doesn't draw out your entire spool. If you're fishing for smaller, weaker fish, set a looser drag. When you pull at the end of your line, the reel should offer a little resistance. If you're fishing for larger, stronger fish, set a tighter drag. You should need to tug firmly at the end of your line to pull more line from the reel.

There is a small dial on the reel (on the side of the closed-face reel, on the top of the open-face reel) that adjusts drag. Tighten it if you find that the fish is pulling line faster than you are reeling it in. Loosen it if your rod is bending and the line is stretching; line *should* unwind from the reel if the fish is really pulling.

〜〜〜〜〜〜〜〜〜〜〜〜〜〜〜〜

that something is a fish, but if you are stream fishing, reeling in, or casting from a moving boat, it could be that a fallen log, a clump of oyster shells, or some other snag is offering you a little action.

Also keep track of your line by touch. Whether you hold the rod in both hands or in one hand, whether you rest the rod in a forked stick or on the edge of a boat, the fishing line is your direct connection to the fish. Learn to trust the hand holding the rod. You'll have to distinguish a fish's presence from the normal weight of the rod, the light pulling of current, the swimming motions of live bait, the slight bouncing of your weight along the bottom. The more you fish, the better you'll be able to interpret these messages.

You'll learn the feel of a fish nibbling and playing, and then the more sudden, stronger, more deliberate movements of a fish's strike. As the fish samples the bait, lunges for it, chomps on it, or sucks it in, the line should say to you, *"Now!"*

Many anglers like to place a finger, lightly touching the line, in front of the reel. That way, the finger itself can feel the line. Your fingertip is sensitive

Small fish, like perch, often nibble the bait.

Predator fish, like walleye, grab the bait.

Bluegill and bass often inhale the bait whole!

to vibrations and will detect even small movements.

This touching is helpful when fishing for smaller fish whose bites make weak signals.

Playing the Fish

Playing a fish means bringing it safely to shore. With a simple pole, the fish is so close to shore you'll just lift or back the pole out of the water. Using a hand-line, you can offer the fish a little more or less line as you lead the fish toward shore. With your rod and reel, however, there are many ways to ensure a good landing.

For sunfish and other small biters, you don't really need to do more than reel in your line. Stronger, larger fish don't always come to shore so easily. These fish need to be "played out" a little. They should be slightly tired before coming to shore.

Stronger fish may run with your line, jump, dive, and turn. If you don't let line out, lower your rod, or adjust your drag; an energetic fish can break your line. This happens most often when an angler yanks too

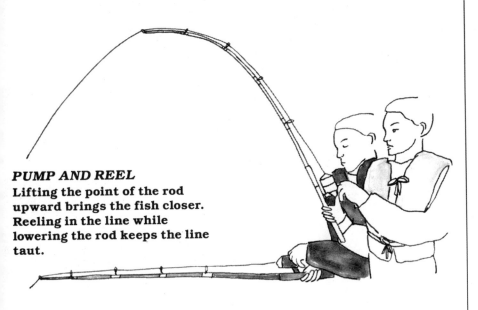

PUMP AND REEL
Lifting the point of the rod upward brings the fish closer. Reeling in the line while lowering the rod keeps the line taut.

hard, reels too fast, or tries to lift a fish straight out of the water while it's struggling.

The best method of bringing in a fish is the "pump-and-reel" method. Each time you feel the fish running with your bait, the line will stretch and the rod will bend. A strong fish might pull line from your reel. When you sense the fish turning or slowing down, you lift the point of the rod upward; that pulls the fish closer. Then you reel in that slackened line and, at the same time, lower the rod toward the water. By

repeating these two moves— lifting the rod, then lowering it and reeling in—you keep the line taut and bring the fish closer.

If you are using an open-face reel, your drag should be tight enough so that when you raise the rod in this pump-and-reel technique, no more line feeds out. If it does, tighten the drag.

In the Weeds

You haven't had a nibble for (what seems like) hours, and so you start to reel in only to discover that your line is:

🐟 snagged among some bottom weeds

🐟 wedged beneath rocks

🐟 wound around a fallen tree

🐟 anchored in a heavy sludge of mud, algae, and shells

🐟 twisted around another angler's cut line

What can you do? First try to work the snag free, pulling the rod or line in one direction and then the other. If you are fishing from shore, walk your line along the bank and try to pull the hook from the opposite direction. If the end of your line is close (let's say you are fishing from a dock), sometimes you can use a long stick or your net to follow the line underwater and pry at the hooked area.

Sometimes all you can do is cut your line free, giving up your hook, sinkers, and lure. This happens to even the most careful angler—the current can move your line into all kinds of messes. But when you know you are near a snaggy, rocky bottom, bait your hook in a "weedless" way that hides its point beneath the bait.

WEEDLESS HOOKS
Many lures and plastic baits have a feather or a wire across the hook's gap to help it avoid snares and snags.

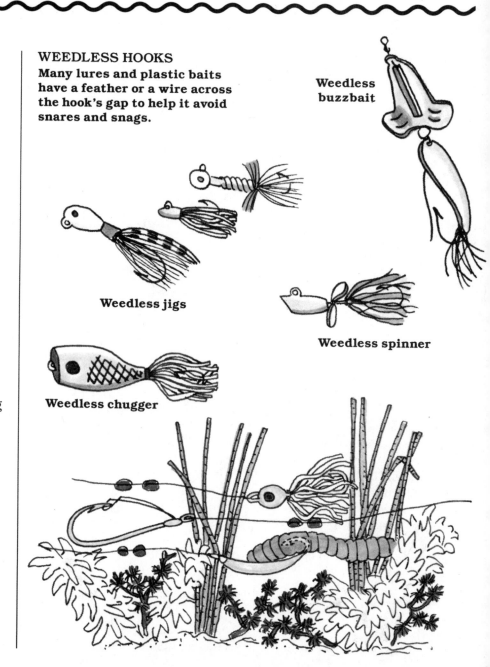

Weedless buzzbait

Weedless jigs

Weedless spinner

Weedless chugger

Think Ecology

If you must cut your line free, remember that this will have a cost. It will not only cost money and tackle, but it might cost a life. Fishing lines often get caught around the feet of shorebirds, cutting or snaring their legs. Sinkers are often swallowed by shorebirds, who die of lead poisoning. Hooks are obviously dangerous. So be an ecological angler. Pick up any old fishing lines you find, and if you think the sunlight has weakened them too much to use, discard them safely. If there are sinkers attached, store them securely in your tackle box.

And since you're looking around your site, pick up any other discarded plastic and fishing litter that you spot and take it home with you. Particularly dangerous to wildlife: six-pack rings, styrofoam, balloons, and other plastics.

About 350 million pounds of fishing gear and packaging materials are lost or dumped by anglers and sailors every year. In that short time, such plastic fishing gear, plastic bags, and wrappers will kill up to a million seabirds, 100,000 sea mammals such as seals and otters, and countless fish.

TEXAS STYLE RIGGING

With live or plastic worms, you can close the gap of your hook by rigging it Texas-style.

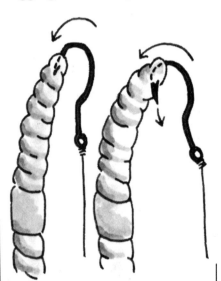

1. Insert the hook into the head end of a worm.

2. Push the hook in about half an inch, and then poke it out through the side of the worm.

3. Slide the rest of the hook into the worm, up to the hook's eye.

4. Twist the hook so that its point now touches the worm.

5. Push the point into the worm, hiding the barb; don't let it punch through to the other side.

Your worm should now hang straight down from your line and slide right through most weedy places.

PLUGS, SPOONS, SPINNERS, JIGS, AND OTHER LURES

A lure is a trick that an angler plays on a fish. It's an unnatural bait (something a fish won't find in the water) made to look like a natural bait (something a fish would find in the water). The angler hopes that the lure will trick the fish into biting. Making or repairing lures is a great fishing hobby on a day too rainy for fishing. Some anglers trade new or antique lures just like other people trade comic books or baseball cards.

Most anglers believe that fishing with lures is more challenging, since the fish has to be tricked into striking. Other anglers say that lures are even more sure-fire than live bait. They are like superbait—even noisier, brighter, sweeter smelling, or more active than the real thing. And all anglers know that lures are always available—no catching needed!—unlike certain kinds of live bait.

But most fish won't be fooled by any old lure acting any old way. An artificial bait must be made to look real. A real crayfish, minnow, or worm knows how to act in the water; an artificial lure made to resemble a crayfish, minnow, or worm doesn't know how to act—unless you control it.

An angler must know how to make the lure imitate the live bait. Would the real food be floating on the surface? Swimming at the bottom? Close to shore? Wiggling, sinking, or swimming? What time of the day and what time of the year would the bait be found?

Because there are all kinds of fish food in the waters, there are all kinds of lures. No angler could possibly use or even be interested in every single lure. Eventually, you'll gather a handful of lures that are just right for the fish you catch at your regular fishing spots.

These thousands of lures have been organized into a few basic types. Some lures whirr or buzz to catch the fish's attention. Some are brightly colored and glitter, sparkle, or flash to catch the fish's eye. Some lures wobble, jiggle, or jump, imitating insects or an injured baitfish. Here are a few common kinds.

Crawler plug

Plugs

are meant to look like small fish. Made of plastic or wood, a plug will float on the surface or sink to the bottom. Plugs often have doll eyes, feathers, small propellers, or wings.

Propbait

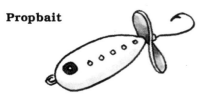

A propbait is a plug with a small twirling propeller on its nose or tail. Largemouth, smallmouth, and striped bass all bite on plugs.

Strategy: Retrieve a plug slowly, in a jerking, twitching fashion across the surface. This creates the gurgling sound of feeding bait fish. You can cover a large area of water pretty quickly by reeling the lure rapidly across the surface. Floating plugs work best when the water is calm and warm. (If the water is too cold, fish won't be in the mood to chase your lure. If there is a lot of current, the fish just won't notice your plug.)

Use a propbait for choppy water since the fish will hear it above the sound of the breaking waves.

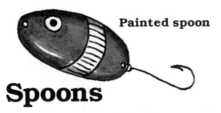

Painted spoon

Spoons

flash and wobble like darting minnows. Most of them are bright metal, sometimes painted or polka-dotted. They spin around as you reel in, attracting a fish with glinting light.

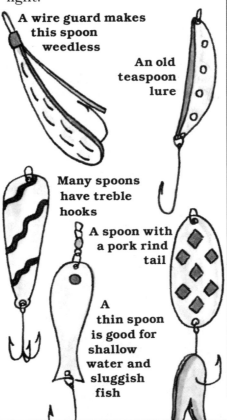

A wire guard makes this spoon weedless

An old teaspoon lure

Many spoons have treble hooks

A spoon with a pork rind tail

A thin spoon is good for shallow water and sluggish fish

Strategy: Tie a swivel on your line to allow the spoon to spin without twisting your line. Clear water is best for spoons, and so is a light monofilament line; heavier line prevents the spoon from wobbling and reflecting. Use a spoon for trout or largemouth bass.

In ponds or shallow water, cast and then slowly reel in the spoon as you feel it drift across the weeds.

TIP

KEEP YOUR SPOONS SHINY AND REFLECTIVE

Dull spoons won't do their job. Rub a tarnished spoon with a damp cloth on which you've sprinkled baking soda. If the spoon won't come clean, try rubbing with steel wool.

Renew or change the color of your spoon by brushing it with fluorescent paint. First paint the spoon with a waterproof white paint; it will help the fluorescent paint adhere.

Spinners

have a single wing or blade that whirls around a wire body making noise and reflecting sunlight. They can be used for most freshwater game fish in clear or cloudy water, and they can be retrieved slowly or quickly. Often spinners have skirts and tails hiding their hooks.

Two standard spinners

Strategy: Retrieving a spinner is very easy, and fish often set the hook themselves on a spinning lure. But don't reel in a spinner at an even speed or some fish will just follow it around without ever striking. Try a few sudden, fast turns of the reel. The fish might grab the lure thinking its "meal" is trying to escape. Use spinners in open water, at shallow or medium depths. And don't forget to attach the spinner to a swivel so that the line doesn't twist.

Jigs

are hooks with a small piece of lead molded below the eye to give shape and weight. They are often decorated with tinsel, feathers, plastic, or strands of hair.

Strategy: Jigs are excellent tackle for weedy areas (since the hooks are partly covered) and for sluggish fish in cold water. Anglers also like jigs for fishing deep at the bottom of a lake.

Rig one of your jigs on your pole or rod, lower the lure into the water and bob it up and down like a fluttering minnow. (See page 28 for jigging tips.)

You can also cast a jig. Aim for a likely spot, allow the jig to sink slowly (watching the whole time), and then reel it in with short skips and hops across the bottom. When you've reeled most of the way in, start again. Some anglers add a small minnow, worm, or insect to the hook of a jig to make it even more attractive to fish.

A bare jig and two dressed jigs

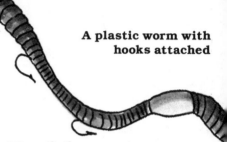

A plastic worm with hooks attached

Rubber or Plastic Lures

are molded to look just like a fish's natural foods—frogs, worms, crayfish, bees, grasshoppers, shrimp, spiders, or other favorites.

Strategy: Most of these lures come without hooks. Simply thread them onto your hook the way you would if they were alive. These are good baits to use for Texas-style rigging; the hook can be tucked inside their soft bodies to avoid snags. Since their soft texture feels more like real food in a fish's mouth, you'll have a bit more time to set a hook before the fish figures out that it has been fooled and spits out the lure.

You can buy plastic worms in all kinds of colors, scents, and sizes. Their tails can be twisted, skirted, or paddle-shaped—each kind provides a different action.

Don't use too much weight on a line baited with a plastic

worm. Your worm will fall too quickly through the water and you might not feel the strike.

Choose a worm only as large or as small as you need for the fish you aim to catch. For instance, a sunfish needs a 2- to 3-inch worm, a smallmouth or spotted bass would like a 4- to 6-inch worm, and a largemouth bass prefers a 6- to 8-inch worm.

A frog and a salamander

As soon as you feel a tug, jerk, tightening, or even slackening in your line, set the hook.

Because the hook is hiding inside that plastic worm, pull hard enough to drive the hook's barb through both the worm and the fish's lip. Use a push-pull movement. Once you feel that fish biting, pull up with the hand that's holding the reel and push away with the hand that's holding the bottom end of the rod. That gives the rod its biggest sweep and sets the hook.

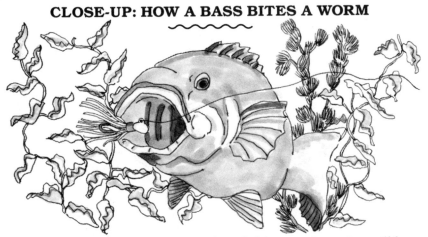

CLOSE-UP: HOW A BASS BITES A WORM

Actually, a bass doesn't *bite* the worm, it sucks it in. If a bass tried to bite, the closing of its mouth would push water ahead of its face, shoving your worm away. (Try clapping your hands underwater, pretending to be a fish's mouth; water will be shoved away by the motion.) To swallow that worm, the fish has to inhale it, and quickly—so quickly that the fish will spit out the worm if it has time to realize that the worm is a fake.

A fringe-tail worm and a crayfish.

Keep your plastic worms soft by storing them in a small plastic bag or bottle. Add a few drops of baby oil and a few drops of vanilla extract. That will also mask the scent of your hands, which might not appeal to the fish.

Flies

are small hooks disguised as insects. Flies are made by tying feathers, yarn, fur, quills, hair strands, or other fuzzy material to very small hooks. Artificial flies are meant to be very light—like insects. To drift in the current or bob on the sur-face, they can't be attached to your regular fishing sinkers. Most anglers use a special rod and reel for fly-fishing that has a weighted line to cast the bait over the water. That equipment is expensive and much easier to master in person, but here are a few adjustments you can make to your spinning rod when fishing with a fly.

FLIES OF EVERY SORT

Depending on the season and the kinds of insects that are breeding or hatching nearby, a fish will eat different kinds of insects. The many types of artificial flies imitate this changing diet.

Dry flies look like floating adult insects. Since they appeal to a fish's eyes, they are used in clear water.

Wet flies, or nymphs, look like sinking insects or newly hatched insects that swim around. They drop slowly under the water.

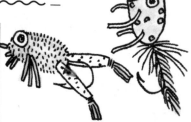

Bugs imitate hard-bodied insects like beetles. There are also mice, frogs, and small baitfish lures called bugs. Anglers fish these baits on top of the water, where they splash, bob, and float. These are good for catching fish that swim in shallow water or just under the surface.

Streamers are bright, flashy lures that are still called flies even though they imitate baitfish. These longer lures are meant for bigger fish. Because they imitate fish, you can fish these lures up or down or across a stream with a slow, fast, jerky, or steady motion.

ADAPT YOUR SPINNING ROD FOR FLY-FISHING

1. Remove the sinkers from your line. Store them in your tackle box.
2. Attach a clear plastic bubble to your line (these can be found at a tackle shop). The fish won't notice the bubble, but it will give your line some weight. Position it like a bobber so it won't interfere with your fly. If you are fishing a "wet fly"— one that sinks—your clear bubble must be far enough from the hook to allow your fly to sink toward the bottom.

In strong current or with very light flies, you might want a little more weight. Add tiny sinkers along your leader, or twist thin, short strips of wire around your line.

FURTHER FISHING ADVENTURES
PART FOUR

When anglers aren't landing a great catch, they're often making their own lures, scheming about the next cast, observing nature, or sketching in a field notebook.

Imagine setting out for a day of saltwater fishing, deep-sea fishing, or ice fishing in winter. There are always new fishing adventures ahead.

MAKING LURES

Below are simple directions for making a few standard lures. After that, you can be creative and invent your own lures. Use your experience, watch other anglers, and wander around the tackle shop for inspiration. Experiment with different materials and colors, combine one idea with another, change patterns and sizes, add an extra tail or feather or scent.

To make the lures included here you'll need:

- pliers
- a file
- a hammer and a small nail with a point about the size of a sharpened pencil
- the hooks and weights from your tackle box
- waterproof paint (model paint, acrylic paint)
- a waterproof, fast-drying superglue
- a small vise. Or try a pinching clothespin that you've nailed or glued to a piece of wood.

PAINTING YOUR LURES

Color a spoon or any other lure with water-proof paint. Before you begin designing your lure, think about the kind of baitfish you are trying to imitate. Check the spoons in your local bait store. Typical spoons might be yellow, red-and-white, polka-dotted, striped, or bearing eyes (at the swivel end, of course, so the lure appears to be swimming in the right direction).

For tying the small threads and knots of flies, use a pair of tweezers with a rubber band to hold the lure tight. If you can have an adult drill a hole into a scrap of lumber, you can fit the tweezers into the wood to secure the vise's grip. Make sure the hole isn't any wider than the widest part of the tweezers. Fold a piece of cardboard between the tips of the tweezers. Insert the bend of a hook in the cardboard. Lock your new vise by inserting the other end of the tweezers into the hole until it fits snugly.

A Spoon

For a spoon lure you will also need:

▶ a silver or stainless steel teaspoon or baby spoon. You can always find spoons at yard sales and junk shops.

▶ 22-gauge stainless steel wire. This is wire that won't rust. Find it at hardware or bait stores.

▶ a swivel

1. Bend the handle of the spoon back and forth until it breaks. (Or ask an adult to help you use a hack saw.) Its edge will be rough; file and hammer it smooth again.

2. With a hammer and a small nail, pierce holes in each end of the spoon. Smooth the rough side of the holes. (An adult can also drill these holes for you.)

3. Cut an inch-long piece of the wire. Loop it through one of the spoon's holes and through the hook's eye.

4. Twist the wire with pliers. Leave a little space (a tiny loop) between the hook and spoon so that the hook can swing freely. After several twists, snip off the extra wire.

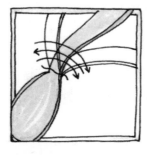

5. Clip your swivel's safety pin into the spoon's other hole.

Try these variations:

🐟 Add a live worm to your spoon's hook. It can make the bait even more tempting.

🐟 Add a rubber tail to the hook: Cut a streamer from a burst balloon. Thread the tail onto the hook so it will wave behind the spoon (see illustration below). You can also use strips of pork rind—the tough outer skin of the meat. Cut inch-long strips of the rind with scissors; keep them in the freezer in a small jar until you need them.

 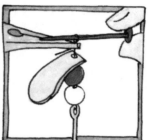 

A Spinner

You'll also need:

🐟 a few small beads (round or square, brightly colored or white, glass or wood). Be sure each bead has a hole large enough for your wire to fit through.

🐟 22-gauge stainless steel wire

🐟 one or two soda can pull-tabs. If you can't find these, use a pair of strong scissors to snip small circles (about 1 inch in diameter) from a stiff aluminum pie plate or a frozen dinner tray. Punch a smooth hole in one end.

🐟 a swivel

🐟 a larger nail

1. Take a 2-inch piece of wire and thread your hook onto it. Slide the hook about half an inch onto the wire and twist the ends together with pliers.

2. Slide a couple of round beads onto the wire, then add one of the spinners. Be sure that the spinner will do what it's supposed to do: spin!

3. Take a larger nail, loop the wire around the nail, and then make three twists in the wire with your pliers. Remove the nail, and you should have a small loop. Snip off the extra wire and attach your swivel to the loop.

Test your spinner to make certain it spins. Attach it to a small piece of string and pull it quickly through clear water. (Try it out in your bathtub.) If it isn't rotating, bend it a little bit in or out, and see what helps the spinner rotate.

Variations for the spinner:

●▶ Add two or three spinners. Separate each one with two or three beads.

●▶ Paint your spinning blades or your beads.

●▶ Add a rubber tail or a skirt around the eye of the hook.

A Jig

You can buy a package of bare jigs at the tackle shop, or you can make your own.

You'll also need:

●▶ some colorful yarn

1. Pinch one of your split-shot sinkers next to the eye of a #4 or #6 hook. Make sure it's attached tightly. (For a #1/0 hook, use a larger [half-ounce] sinker.)

2. Paint the sinker white, red, or yellow. Dab a dot of black on each side to give the jig two eyes. Let the jig dry.

3. Take a 6-inch piece of yarn that matches the paint. Hold the yarn along the shank of the hook so that only about an inch of yarn is lower than the hook's bottom bend. You'll use that inch to finish the knot.

4. Wrap the yarn around the hook starting just underneath your sinker. Loop it around and around the hook as tightly as you can. Once the shank is covered, hold the yarn in place with your finger and thumb.

5. Take the extra end of yarn hanging by the bend and make a double knot with your two ends. Add a drop of waterproof glue and let it dry.

6. Leave half an inch of yarn to wiggle behind the lure.

Try a few variations:

●▶ Add a small downy feather alongside the shank before you complete the wrapping of yarn. (You can usually find these small feathers on the ground.) Let the feather partially hide the hook to make it weedless.

●▶ Add other skirts or streamers such as a snippet of doll's hair, Christmas tinsel, "hair" from an old Halloween mask, or a few strands from an old paintbrush. Add these under the yarn behind the jig's head or add them to the rear, around the hook.

●▶ Add an extra tail to the jig by gluing on a small piece of a plastic worm. Slide the worm onto the hook where your yarn is dangling free, but don't cover the hook completely.

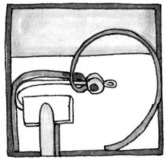

A Bug

For this great bug you'll also need:

- a small cork, about the size of the first joint on your finger. Buy these at the tackle shop, or find an old wine cork (that hasn't been torn up by the corkscrew). One wine cork can provide the "bodies" for two or three bugs.

- a sharp knife

- two medium-thickness rubber bands

- a short feather (about an inch long). A blue jay, cardinal, gull, or any other long flight feather can be cut into several pieces.

1. Ask an adult for help. Using a sharp knife, cut a slot into the cork. The slot should be one-quarter inch deep—a third of the way through the cork.

2. Add a drop of glue to your hook's shank, and slide it inside this slot. Leave the eye poking above the fatter end. Depending on the size of the cork, you'll probably need a #4 or #6 hook. A little of the shaft and the whole bend of the hook should stick out from the narrower end of the cork. Pry open the channel if you can and add another drop of glue. Let the bug dry.

3. Paint the cork in a way that resembles an insect you think your local fish might like. Yellow, black, red, or white? Stripes or dots? Add a pair of eyes. Let the paint dry.

4. Take your small nail and poke two shallow holes on each side of the cork and one in the back, above the hook's bend.

5. Cut rubber strips from your rubber bands. You want the straight—not the curved—

parts. Use the same nail to apply a dot of waterproof glue to each cork hole. Then use the nail to poke a piece of rubber band into each hole.

6. Apply a dot of glue to your small feather and insert the feather into the hole above the hook at the back of the bug.

Try these variations:

- Use a small piece of sponge instead of the cork. Since sponge is softer in the fish's

---

TIP

NAME THAT LURE!

Give each new lure you create a special name! Find a name that describes the lure's action or tells where you invented it. Name it for one of your angling friends, or the place where you first used it. Here are the wacky names of some commercial lures: Erie Dearie, Paddle Wacker, Devil's Toothpick, Rat-L-Stik, Mister Twister Keeper, Dina-Mite, Jelly Belly, Wob-L-Rite, Junior Flutterdevle, Moss Boss, Fur Ant.

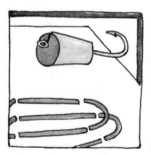

mouth, it often fools more fish. (Don't paint the sponge, but otherwise follow the same steps.)

▶ Try other arrangements of "arms" and "legs" and "tails."

▶ Instead of rubber legs, insert little strands of feather around the head or base of your bug. Give it a fuzzy pair of wings to imitate a moth. Try a pair of rubber strips at the back of the plug to imitate a frog.

A Basic Fly

Since flies are much smaller than the other lures we've made, be sure to use a vise.

You'll also need:

▶ a #6 hook, for starters. Most anglers tie flies that are much smaller than a #6, but small flies take practice.

▶ a spool of nylon thread, preferably black

1. With your hook secured in your vise, take about two feet of nylon thread and tie a knot around the shank of the hook just below the eye. Cut off any extra thread dangling from the short end.

2. Wind the thread neatly along the whole shank of the hook. Cover the hook so that nothing shows through the thread's winding. Stop wrapping when you reach the bend.

3. Add a piece of yarn—red or yellow—along the shaft. Leave a quarter inch to hang below the bend. Now wrap the thread around the yarn five or six times until you are back at the hook's eye. (The yarn is supposed to show through the thread wrappings.) Make a knot in the thread to hold the yarn in place.

MAKE A SIMPLE BOBBER

The best homemade bobbers are empty thread spools, especially the light plastic ones. Simply paint the bobber to make it easy to watch. Red or yellow offer the most contrast to the blue-green water.

Thread your line through the spool. Fix the bobber at the right place on your line by tucking a toothpick or a stick—whatever makes a snug fit—into the spool's hole. Pull out the stick to adjust the bobber and the bait's depth.

A wine cork will also make a fine bobber if an adult drills a hole all the way through its length.

4. Place a small, stiff feather along the shaft. Wrap the thread around its end several times. Now skip a few strands of the feather and wrap the thread a few times around it; skip a few more strands, then wrap again. The idea is to make the feather's hairs stand out in bunches.

5. When you reach the eye of the hook and the whole shaft is bound with thread, use up most of the thread by wrapping until you've formed a small ball— that will be the "head" of your fly. Make two secure knots. Cut off any extra thread. Add a drop of glue.

This fly is called a "black woolly worm." Fly-tying is a real art; some anglers spend a great deal of time tying a whole range of unusual flies.

Try these variations:

🐟 Shape the feathers on your fly in different ways. Try to make a pair of wings when you wrap the feather. Add a few wisps of feather for a tail to hang behind the bend of the hook.

🐟 For wet flies, the kind that sink below the surface, add bigger snippets of feathers. Try different colors and different shapes. Make the body out of yarn instead of thread.

🐟 For even bigger flies like streamers, use bigger hooks and whole, large feathers.

If you really enjoy tying flies, you'll find many books in the library devoted to this craft.

FISH THAT FISH

Fringed goosefish

Anglerfish

the pole

the bait

the trap!

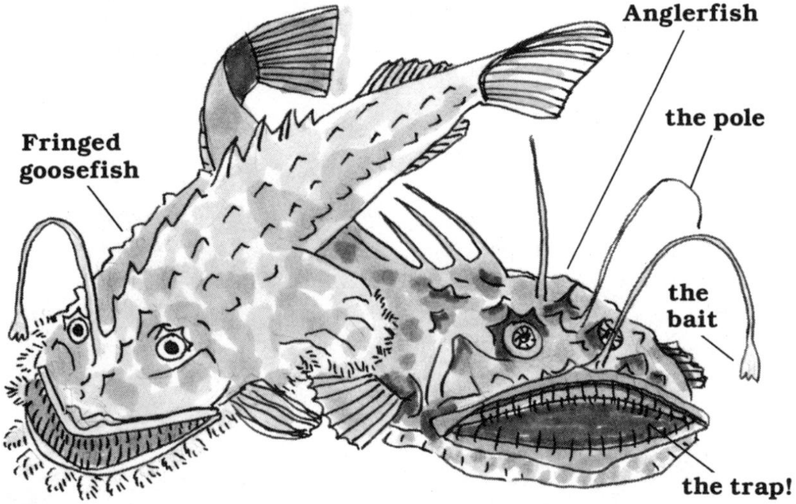

At some mysterious point in their evolution, certain fish grew their own "fishing gear" and learned to fish. These fish are called anglerfish. One of the anglerfish's dorsal spines separated from the rest of the fin, slid down to the fish's snout, lengthened into a rod, thinned out into a line, and then formed a little worm-like bait at its tip. Waiting very still, an anglerfish dangles its "bait" in front of its mouth. As soon as an unwary fish comes close enough to take the bait, the anglerfish opens its mouth and sucks in the curious fish. No removing a hook! No net! No filleting or scaling or cooking!

AN ANGLER IN THE ECOSYSTEM

A skilled, careful, responsible angler remembers that fish are living, breathing creatures that participate in a complicated environment called an ecosystem. An ecosystem is made of everything—and nothing can be left out!—that belongs to one particular place. One pond. One inlet of the ocean. One part of a creek. One forest. It includes all plants, animals, insects, rocks, and soils in that place, as well as seasonal things such as rain and temperature. Each element is an essential, working contributor to that ecosystem.

Every fish *needs* food and every fish *is* food. This is a balance that Nature maintains. But since we humans have taken so much land and water for our own buildings, farms, and industries, we have also taken the responsibility to help Nature maintain these important balances. For example, in a watery ecosystem, larger fish keep the population of small fish from getting too abundant. Small fish regulate the population of insects on the water's surface. Trees along the riverbank provide shade and keep the sun from overheating the water. The waters, the forests, the fields—all these are carefully balanced ecosystems.

So just as a tree that falls in a stream will change the fish's swimming patterns, the water's current, and the amount of sunlight and shade, an angler can also make a change in that ecosystem. A smart angler knows how many and what kinds of fish to take to help maintain the balance.

Every state passes laws to tell anglers their part in that season's balance. They try to ensure that there are never too many or too few of each kind of fish.

WARNING

POISON PLANTS

The more you move around in a field or woods, the more chances you'll have of encountering some kind of irritating plant. Be sure you can identify poison ivy, poison oak, and poison sumac. If you do think one of these plants has touched your skin, wash as soon as you can with hot water and a strong soap, such as Fels-Naptha.

Recognize poison ivy by its trio of shiny bright green leaves that are pointed and jagged.

In autumn, the leaves turn red-orange and the plant bears red berries.

Poison oak has white berries and three-lobed leaflets.

Poison sumac.

Even though you are only one angler, there are so many millions of other people taking fish from the water that you become part of a very powerful force for change. What each individual personally adds to or takes from the water can be critical to an ecosystem.

Meanwhile, While You're Fishing

It's a beautiful day, you've found the perfect spot for fishing, your favorite angling partner is beside you, and the fish are ... well ... not exactly jumping onto the hook. Of course, you'll try other spots and other baits, but why not break up the day with other fun things that go hand-in-hand with fishing.

Be an active angler. Don't just wait, plot! Think about the next lure or change of bait. Watch the water for clues to where the fish are hiding and eating.

Read. There isn't a better place for reading than beside the water. Why not take a book of fishing stories? Or a book about your favorite fish? There are library shelves devoted just to trout, bass, bay fish—you name it.

Observe. Look and listen. There are the sounds of birds and insects; there are blooming wildflowers and water plants; there's a canopy of trees and a dense underbrush brimming with life. Portable field guides can help you identify the songbirds, wildflowers, trees, or shells in your area. Go on a nature walk. Start a list of the species you encounter. Sketch, photograph, or keep a field notebook.

Some other favorite things for angling hours:

- Make a few lures.
- Clean or repair your tackle.
- Whittle.
- Collect shells, beach glass, or driftwood.

HOW TO SKIP A STONE

Do people all over the world, on the shore of every body of water, enjoy skipping stones? How many times will the stone skip before it sinks?

Before you skip stones, move to a part of the water where you won't disturb other anglers. Skipping stones spooks nearby fish.

Find a flat, silver-dollar-size stone. Grab the stone around its edges with your first finger and your thumb. You'll be making a circle around the stone and balancing it underneath with your middle finger. Using the sidearm cast (see page 60), throw the stone parallel to the water so that it slides across the surface. Bend your elbow, holding your forearm and hand even with the ground, and then bring your hand forward, throwing the rock straight out onto the water. Let your first finger give the final boost.

If the stone went far out over the water before skipping, try to aim the next stone lower, closer to the water.

If the stone hit the water and immediately sunk, try to aim the next stone higher, a little farther away from the shore.

Three, eight, twelve skips? Have a contest with your friends or with yourself. What will your all-time skipping record be?

That's a Keeper

There are many ways to keep a fish besides in a creel or inside your stomach. The poet Robert Frost once said that "strongly spent" is nearly the same thing as "kept." If you really feel something—really use all your senses, really give your heart and your best thinking and your talents—then even a brief and quick experience, such as catching a fish, is kept. *Strongly spend* your time while fishing and you do the same thing as keeping the fish.

In this way, you can have the fish and still let the fish have its freedom. You can save the memory of that fish and still save the fish's life. Here are some other ways of "keeping" fish:

Log book. Many anglers keep a record of all the fish they have ever caught. Record all kinds of information, as shown in the illustration. These details will not only help you remember your great catches, but you can use them to plan your next, better and wiser day of fishing.

Measurements. Take a quick measurement of your fish before you release it. Use a flexible measuring tape (the kind used in sewing), since it doesn't have sharp edges. Keep your hands wet, keep the fish in the water, and quickly place the tape from the side of its mouth to the tip of its tail.

Pictures. Take a photograph or make a quick sketch of your catch. You'll need a fishing buddy to help with this. If you use a camera, have your partner lift the fish out of the water at the moment when you are ready to shoot. Leave the hook in the fish's mouth, and lift the fish with the line. Then remove the hook and begin your release.

If you have a sketchbook, you'll need a holding tank— your cooler minus the ice—to hold your fish for a few minutes. Remove the hook, place the fish in your water-filled holding tank, and begin a rough sketch. Just get down the basics. Write down the colors you'll want to add later. Note any interesting markings or patterns. Then release the fish correctly. Complete the sketch at home, adding details, colors, and descriptions.

Life list. Each time you catch a new kind of fish, add it

to your "life list." If you don't know what kind of fish you caught, ask someone at the tackle shop or compare your sketch or your memory of the fish to pictures in a fishing book.

Story. Every angler has stories—true fishing stories and what we'll call "fishy" fishing stories: the story of The One That Got Away; the story of The Biggest Fish in This Lake; the story of The Stubbornest, Wiliest, Wisest, Shrewdest, Hungriest Fish That Ever... (you fill in the blanks). Fishing stories have been around since the first human cast a line into the water, caught a fish, lost a fish, and came home to tell somebody. Each time you share a fishing story with a friend, you're keeping that fish in a story.

MAKE A FISH PRINT

If you've decided to cook the fish, another way to "keep" it is by making a fish print of the catch before you clean it. You need:

🐟 food coloring or, for a subtler print, cooking oil

🐟 a piece of blank paper larger than your fish

1. Brush the food coloring or oil (in one direction only) on one side of the fish. Coat it lightly but completely.

2. Place the paper on top of the painted fish. Firmly press the paper along its entire surface. Don't forget the edges or the fins. If your paper is very stiff, first mist the top side with water.

3. Take one corner of the paper and peel the paper from the fish. If the print didn't come out the way you'd like, try again using more or less coloring, or a lighter or heavier paper.

If you really want a beautiful record of the fish, use very little food coloring and make a light fish print. Let the paper dry, then color in the fish's true details with pencils or crayons. Now add some information to the print: its name, the length of the fish, and where and when you caught it. Once the fish print dries, iron out any wrinkles (place a blank sheet of paper over your print before ironing).

FISHING FARTHER OUT AND COMING HOME

Saltwater game fish are usually larger, heavier, and more dangerous than freshwater fish. Anglers often need bigger, more expensive equipment, and often, a powerboat. The miles of salt water bordering our coasts have many specialized and variable ecosystems. So many things influence the kinds of fish and fishing in a particular saltwater spot: depth, current, amount of salt, wind, available foods, predators.

Saltwater conditions vary so much that the same kind of fish can be commonly found as a 1-pounder off the shoreline of one state—and as an 80-pounder farther out to sea! Since there are more than 30 times more saltwater than freshwater fish on earth, there are also more specialized ways of catching saltwater fish. The best all-around strategy is to seek some local advice from tackle shops, experienced anglers, or regional magazines. You'll want to know what kinds of fish you can catch in your area with your equipment. If you are using a hand-line or a pole, you'll be casting for spot, surfperch, black sea bass, flounder, or crabs. With a rod and reel you can reach a little farther out, and a little deeper. If you have friends or family to take you on a powerboat, a fishing charter boat, or even a rowboat, you'll have the chance to troll or drift for an even wider range of fish.

Fish You'll Meet in Salt Water

Here are species of fish found up and down the Atlantic and Pacific coasts, as well as in the Gulf of Mexico. The average weights and lengths for most of these fish vary widely. But in general, if you are fishing close to shore with your #1/0 hook and 4- to 6-pound line, your catch is likely to be between 6 and 18 inches long, and from 6 ounces to 2 pounds in weight.

Saltwater sportfishing is usually regulated very carefully by each state because so many of these fish are caught commercially. Many have been over-

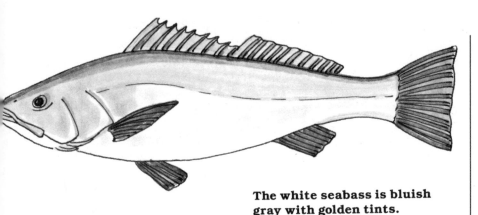

The white seabass is bluish gray with golden tints.

fished and are legal to catch only during certain months. Your source of local advice, a tackle shop, or the state department of wildlife will help you understand any restrictions.

DRUM

Along the Atlantic shores, the drum family provides many favorites for anglers. The names "drum" and "croaker" come from the drumming sound the male fish creates with the muscles around its swim bladder. The red drum is copper colored with a black spot at the tail's base. It can weigh up to 80 pounds, but most anglers take 15- to 40-pound drums. The commonest drum, the silver- or bronze-colored Atlantic croaker, averages 2 to 4 pounds. Along the Pacific coast lives another

favorite member of the drum family, the white seabass.

Strategy: Smaller croakers and white seabass can be caught by casting into the surf with a heavily weighted line or by bottom-fishing from a boat. Fishing for drum is a great

chance to join other anglers on a boating trip. Typical baits for drum are saltwater minnows, alewives, and soft pieces of crab.

FLOUNDER

Fishing from the shore, a small boat, or even a dock during an incoming tide, an angler can try for one of the tastiest fish of all: the flounder. While most of the fish we're likely to catch will be 1 or 2 feet long, some members of this family, like the halibut, grow to 8 feet long and 4 feet wide. Can you imagine a flat 300-pound fish?

Most flatfish live on the ocean floor, feeding on shellfish, sand eels, and minnows.

Strategy: Be sure the bait sinks to the bottom. Tie your

The red drum is copper colored with a black spot at the tail's base.

hook on a 12-inch leader so that it hangs about 8 inches above your plummet sinker (see page 37). You'll feel lots of bumping as the sinker travels along the sand. Wait for that sudden, deliberate tug that means a bite. (Telling a bump from a bite will take some practice, but you'll get the hang of it, even if you reel in a few extra times just to be sure.)

Keep your bait moving with the incoming tide. That is how a flounder feeds. If you cast from the shore, let the bait drift in with the incoming current. Cast out frequently. If you are trolling from a boat, let your line drift behind as the boat is carried with the current.

A FRESHWATER RINSE FOR SALTWATER TACKLE

Salt water is hard on all fishing gear. Salt corrodes metal, weakens plastic and rubber, and leaves a crusty deposit of salt and sand on everything. Give your tackle a fresh water rinse with a hose after salt water fishing.

Most anglers use small saltwater minnows, pieces of eel, mussels, or pieces of soft crab. You'll need a #1/0 hook. If you plan on doing lots of flounder fishing, buy a slightly larger hook (#2/0 to #4/0) with a long shank to make hook removal easier.

BLACK SEA BASS/ SPOT/PERCH

The many members of these families occupy most of the close-to-shore saltwater niches. You'll be likely to find the 1-pound, 12-inch variety in nearly every bay and inlet of the United States. Of course.

Most flounders are spotted brown and black and gray on one side. On the side that faces the bottom, the skin is white.

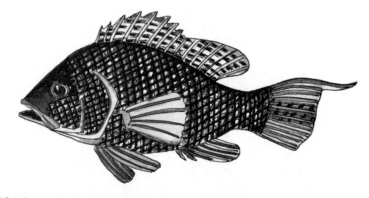

The black seabass is olive, black, brown, or gray with a whiter underbelly and a pointed, S-curving tail.

larger members might be lurking nearby, so be ready for anything.

Strategy: Here's where local advice will really help you identify the right bait and the right tackle. Try cut fish, or squid, soft crab pieces, bloodworms, or nightcrawlers. Use your #1/0 hook, a little heavier line (8- to 10-pound-test) if you have it, and rig your line with the double leader (on page 37). In strong current, you might want to buy a heavier plummet (½- or ¾-ounce).

The spot's scales are metallic-looking, silver or bluish gray, with a large black spot behind the gill cover.

The Atlantic croaker is silver or bronze colored.

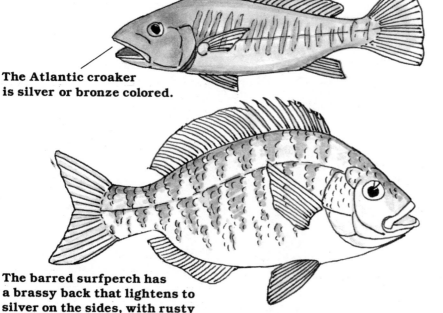

The barred surfperch has a brassy back that lightens to silver on the sides, with rusty brown bars.

RECORD WEIGHTS FOR SALTWATER FISH

Here are a few record fish caught on a rod and reel in the salt waters of America. Some of the heaviest fish ever caught are listed here:

Black sea bass   **1979**
Wt: 8 pounds 12 ounces
Oregon Inlet, NC

Bluefish   **1972**
Wt: 31 pounds 12 ounces
Hatteras Inlet, NC

Summer flounder   **1975**
Wt: 22 pounds 7 ounces
Montauk, NY

Jewfish   **1961**
Wt: 680 pounds
Fernandina Beach, FL

Blue Atlantic marlin   **1977**
Wt: 1282 pounds
St. Thomas, V.I.

Spotted sea trout   **1977**
Wt: 16 pounds
Mason's Beach, VA

Bluefin tuna   **1979**
Wt: 1496 pounds
Aulds Cover, N.S., Canada

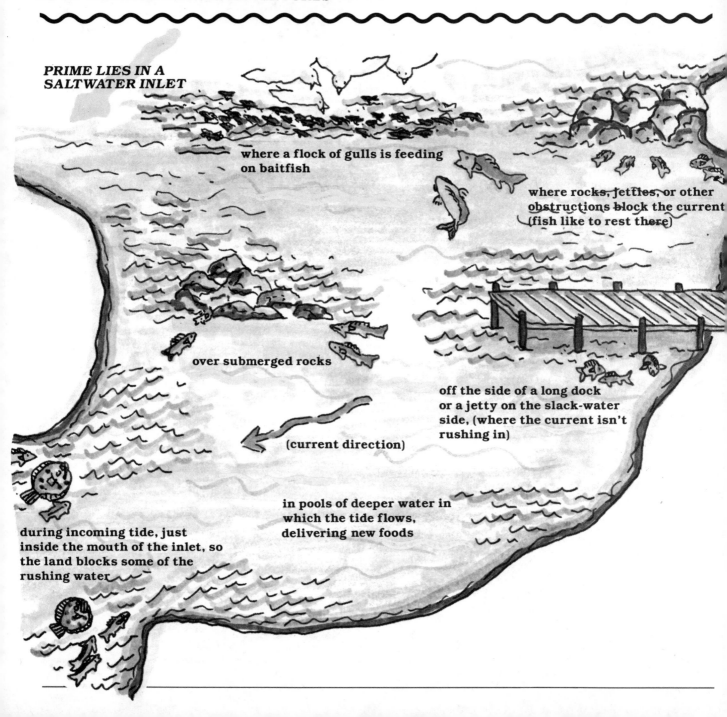

*PRIME LIES IN A
SALTWATER INLET*

where a flock of gulls is feeding
on baitfish

where rocks, jetties, or other
obstructions block the current
(fish like to rest there)

over submerged rocks

off the side of a long dock
or a jetty on the slack-water
side, (where the current isn't
rushing in)

(current direction)

in pools of deeper water in
which the tide flows,
delivering new foods

during incoming tide, just
inside the mouth of the inlet, so
the land blocks some of the
rushing water

The Fish You've Caught to Eat

The key to great-tasting fresh fish is to prepare and eat your catch as soon as possible. If you can't cook the fish right away, rinse it under fresh running water, wrap it in waxed paper, and refrigerate it. (Of course, if you can't cook the fish that same hour or that same day, you can freeze it. But what's the point of eating fresh fish if the fish is no longer fresh?)

Smaller fish, such as sunfish, crappie, bass, and walleye, need only to be scaled and gutted; larger fish need to be filleted so they will cook more quickly and evenly. Filleting a fish takes some practice and a very sharp knife. Ask an adult

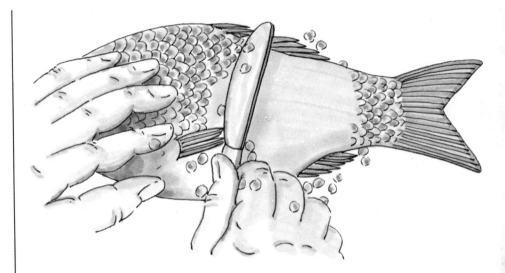

to do it for you the first few times.

Fish with no scales (like catfish) or only tiny scales (like trout), need only to be gutted; either the flesh will slide off the skin while cooking, or it can be gently removed on the plate.

Look in any good cookbook for basic fish recipes—the simpler, the better!

SCALING A FISH

A fish's scales are easy to remove, but they can create a mess. You can end up with clear, pearly dots everywhere— on your hands, face, countertops, and floor. So scale your fish under running water, preferably outdoors.

1. Hold the fish down on a flat surface and let water run gently over the fish.
2. Take a dull butter knife, spoon, or fish scaler, and scrape the fish from the tail toward the head. The scales should come right off.
3. Scrape both sides and the back. (There aren't many scales on a fish's belly.)

If you've been using the kitchen sink, be sure to empty the scales from the strainer into the garbage.

GUTTING A FISH

1. Place the fish on a few layers of newspaper. (Once you have finished, fold the paper around the discarded parts, and toss it into the trash.)

2. Using a sharp knife, slit the belly from the vent to the pelvic fins. The cut doesn't need to be deep. You'll find all the inside organs shown on page 11. Your knife can help prod these from the body cavity. There should be nothing inside but the lining surrounded by the fish's ribs and backbone. Slit the membrane that covers the backbone and remove the blood vessel from this cavity.

3. Rinse well.

In many recipes, you cook the fish just like this. Of course, you can remove the head, tail, and fins. Use a sharp knife and simply slice them off.

FISHY HANDS

After fishing, and especially after cleaning fish, your hands will smell like fish. If soap doesn't remove the odor, sprinkle baking soda on your wet hands, rub vigorously, and rinse. Then wash with soap again. Rubbing a slice of lemon over your skin will also help.

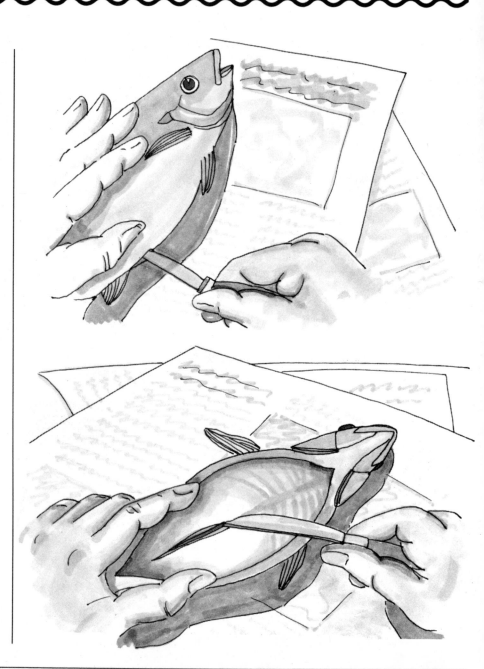

Fishing Farther from Home

Once you're hooked on fishing, you may want to explore many other techniques that anglers have invented.

The biggest adventure is a new place to fish. If you're lucky enough to vacation in other parts of the country, visit the local fishing spots. Just as the geography will be different, so will the fishing—there will probably be new fish for your life list.

Someday you might go fishing on a boat. You'll be able to fish deeper and farther from shore. You'll have a chance to troll from a moving boat, to motor quietly into narrow inlets, or to speed into the open water where larger game fish are feeding.

Surfcasting at the ocean can be thrilling. There, you cast with long rods into the waves along a shoreline where smaller game fish are feeding. It takes a lot of strength and strong equipment to land large game fish.

Many anglers enjoy wading with long hip boots into a

stream. Trout and salmon anglers get right into the moving water and use special fly-casting rods. It's slippery business, and something you should do with an experienced adult.

There's ice fishing, too. Northern anglers have learned the careful method of walking out on frozen lakes and ponds and jigging their lines through a hole cut in the ice. It's a strange and wonderful experience for anglers who live where water freezes to a safe depth. *Don't attempt this without a very experienced ice-angler at your side.*

Maybe that charter boat will take you deep-sea fishing, where the game fish are truly powerful, beautiful—and sometimes dangerously outfitted with teeth, swords, fins, and spines. These fish are so powerful, you might have to be strapped into a chair so you won't be pulled overboard! Some anglers have joined an important study in fish ecology; when they catch a deep-sea fish, they implant a small, harmless tag in the fish's tail, then release it. The tag can track the fish's growth, the distance it has migrated, and other important facts.

With all these other kinds of fishing, you'll need an adult's help and you'll need special tackle. Most anglers are happy to let you use their equipment once you've been invited along for the trip. They'll have all the advice you need, complete with tricks, the right lures, and new techniques.

YOUR OWN BACKYARD

Many anglers never travel farther than a favorite creek or inlet, and never do any kind of fishing except casting small lures and live bait. They like to fish, day after familiar day, at their own local fishing spots.

But every kind of fishing offers you the same great mix of experiences: peace and quiet that's full of excitement; facts about fishing science balanced by lots of practical experience; good physical coordination but also a lot of unrehearsed luck; a chance to deepen your curiosity as well as your concern for the other living creatures who share this planet; a block of time to spend alone or with your favorite angling friends.

Leave Only Footprints: Take Only Pictures

Those are the words of a sign that should be posted in every place where you might be fishing. Unless you plan to eat the day's catch, in which case you'll be taking home a certain number of fish of a legal size, leave your fishing site as if you had never been there. Make your visit disappear. Bring away only what your eyes took by looking, what your ears caught by hearing, what your nose gathered by smelling.

Take pictures—in your mind, in a story, in a camera, or in a sketchbook. But otherwise, come and go like a guest in Nature's house. Be careful not to trample the grasses and wildflowers along your way. Take home all paper and plastic and glass that you've brought and pick up any litter left from other people's carelessness. Be careful not to put anything into the water that doesn't belong there.

You keep every fish you've ever caught and every fish that got away in your memory. You may have released those fish, but the memories of those experiences still swim around inside your head. And once you've caught a memory, you can't release it even if you try.

INDEX